52 Leadership Gems

Practical and Quick Insights for Leading Others

John Parker Stewart

J.P. Stewart Systems, Inc.
PO Box 1527, Lake Oswego, OR 97035
503.638.1106
www.johnparkerstewart.com

Published by Leadership Excellence
www.LeaderExcel.com

Library of Congress Cataloging-in-Publication Data

ISBN: 978-1-930771-38-3

Printed in the United States of America

Also by John Parker Stewart:

LEAD NOW! A Personal Leadership Coaching Guide for Results-Driven Leaders

52 Leadership Lessons: Timeless Stories for the Modern Leader

Winning Orals: The Master Formula for Securing Government Contracts

Advance Praise

"John Parker Stewart's *52 Leadership Gems* is a wonderful compilation of leadership tips and insights vital to leaders and managers at any level. He provides invaluable guidance that will help leaders and managers build a successful career."

Chris Jedrey, former Executive Director,
NASA Headquarters

"*52 Leadership Gems* is a must read for all managers who wish to continuously improve their management skills. It is one of the most compelling books on leadership in years. John Parker Stewart has successfully condensed 35 years of executive training and coaching to provide insight and practical advice into a common sense format to enable managers to achieve success and prepare for future uncertainties in today's competitive marketplace."

Bill Gillan, Chief Operating Officer, Dynanet Corp

"I have had the privilege of attending several of John Parker Stewart's leadership sessions over the years. Consistently, the aspect that resonates with all participants are the 'Gems' that John shares. For those who have not had the good fortune to witness this first hand, *52 Leadership Gems* is the next best thing. Enjoy the *Gems* and pass them on."

Kenneth S. Reightler, Jr.,
former Astronaut and Space Shuttle Pilot
former president of Lockheed Martin Space Operations

"*52 Gems* is a fantastic collection of leadership wisdom presented in a short, condensed format that makes them an easy-to-use reference guide. I am carrying it in my work bag alongside my laptop everyday so that I can have proper food for thought! John taught them to my entire executive team and we referred to them often as pillars of our corporate culture. John is a world-class coach—the best one there is"

Tarek Robbiati, former CEO of CSL, Hong Kong
Current GMD and Chairman,
Telstra International Group, Asia

"Having employed John Parker Stewart as a Leadership Team Trainer several times in the past 25 years, I can assure you that what he shares in *52 Leadership Gems* are quick insights for leading others that really work. Many were captured from John's experience transforming and building my very successful Leadership Teams. John has extracted the key points from his training of over 10,000 students in becoming successful supervisors, managers and executives. The format is easy to follow—filled with proven advice that is easy to understand, to recall and to apply. This is one of the most, practical books on leadership I have seen in years. These *Gems* will be very helpful to you and your management team in leading your organization in its climb to new heights of success."

Bill Brett, Senior Executive,
Kennedy Space Center, Florida
Johnson Space Center, Houston

"*52 Leadership Gems* provides the essential information for bringing your career to the next level. Looking inside the mind of John Parker Stewart is like having an encyclopedia for executives in your hip pocket. Imagine having 30 years of wisdom geared toward the consolidated knowledge of a brilliant and insightful executive coach available to you in a handy, organized, easy to use guide."

Ben Bartine, Director of Delivery, CIBER

"An extremely useful collection of easy-to-read and practical insights to guide you through your every day, challenging leadership situations. Practicing these insightful *52 Leadership Gems* will guarantee that you and your team will excel as leaders and managers. John Parker Stewart taught us these gems as he coached us through the challenges of constant change that all executives are facing today."

Jack Nealon, Former Chief Information Officer,
National Agricultural Statistics Service,
U.S. Department of Agriculture

"John Parker Stewart has provided a way to solve every challenge facing organizations today. Move over *One Minute Manager* here comes *52 Leadership Gems*—An essential guide for every leader for what to do next. Keep this book in your top desk drawer, you will find it invaluable. In time of crisis, pull it out and you will find your answer. John has done a masterful job of providing an amazing amount of help in an accessible, quick to use guide. It is an outstanding handbook by an exceptional executive coach!"

Rob Roe, former Sr Executive, IBM
former Director Sales and Marketing, Telstra
current Managing Director, Air-watch,
Australia & New Zealand

Dedication

Dedicated to my good friend and colleague, Tarek Robbiati and his exceptional team at CSL in Hong Kong. You knew these gems so well that you all referred to them in your meetings and day-to-day work by their number!

Acknowledgments

Over the years I have traveled the globe working with leaders in countless varieties of challenges. I dedicate these *Gems* to those thousands of leaders who have shown me that leadership can be taught and learned, thereby achieving extraordinarily satisfying results *through others*! They have demonstrated my philosophy that the only way you can succeed is by helping your people succeed.

There are many who have supported and encouraged me in my research, consulting and coaching over the years. These include my clients, staff, editors, friends, associates, and my family.

In particular, I salute and honor my wife for her sustaining and constant support, encouragement and patience with my crazy schedule, work, travel, and research. To Debra, I give my love and gratitude!

I offer my sincere appreciation to my clients for the experiences they have given me in the role of "laboratory," allowing me to experiment and test my theories—usually successfully.

Some of the most satisfying learning and associations came from my consulting, teaching, and coaching opportunities with:

- Lockheed Martin—13 years in developing, designing and teaching the Lockheed Martin Executive Institutes. CEOs Roy Anderson and Dan Tellep, you are class acts!

- NASA—12 years in teaching the leaders of Kennedy Space Center, who achieved an award fee score of "100" for the first time in their history. Well done, Jay Honeycutt! What challenges—both tragic and joyful—we witnessed and overcame!

- Toshiba, and the unique executive training sessions we had in the classroom and mountains with you, Tom Levitt.

- Telstra—Sydney and Melbourne—Coaching the Executive Leadership Programs.

- United Space Alliance—working with CEO Kent Black and COO Jim Adamson in developing their executive team in the "early" years of the Lockheed Martin, Rockwell, Boeing venture.

- CSL-Hong Kong—coaching and training Tarek Robbiati's senior team. What a pleasure to coach your team individually and collectively as we had offsites in China and Macau. You guys sure knew these *Gems*!

- Pacific Bell (Verizon)—coaching and training all managers in network engineering and sales for three years. Chuck Hensley, we made a huge difference!

- Idaho National Engineering Lab—5 years in coaching and developing all of management as you experienced major change initiatives. Beth Britt, it was a genuine pleasure!

- Johnson Space Center in Houston—simultaneously working with every major contractor in supporting the shuttle operations. Bill Brett of Raytheon, what a time we had!

- US Dept of Ag NASS—coaching and executive development with the SES Team. Dr. Clark, you had more challenges thrown at you than any previous administrator!
- National Institute for Internal Auditors—Training and Developing Leadership Skills. Those weekly sessions were long and tough—but so worth it!

I also express appreciation to my wife, Debra, and to our four sons—Daniel, Peter, Jared and Brian—for their always willing, drop-of-a-hat support for anything I ever needed.

My son, Daniel, was an exceptional writing partner through the entire process. It was a father's joy to have such a privilege!

I sincerely thank Ken Shelton and Allan Jensen for their tireless and patient help, support, knowledge, experience, judgment and professionalism in editing this work. It was a pleasure to work with them and Leadership Excellence as we completed and published the book. They were always encouraging and most helpful in countless ways!

Finally, to my highly skilled and very capable in-house editor, Megan Wilcken, I acknowledge with highest praise and appreciation all your work. You made it happen!

Contents

I am still learning.

— Michelangelo

Introduction

For the past three decades I have taught leadership and management sessions to organizations all over the globe. The audience has spanned CEOs, presidents, political leaders, military commanders, professors, supervisors, students and parents, church groups, and community organizations. The time I had with them ranged from a few hours in a conference or convention to several weeks in an intensive executive development session. In each case, I found that the best way for my audience to remember a key point I was making, in a story or example, was to give them a "gem." The gem encapsulated the essence of the lesson. I encouraged them to write the gem down for later reference to help them recall the core message. It worked. I have been amazed how people recalled gems many years after I had taught them in a class or conference.

Many of the "students" kept a list of these gems and passed them on, one at a time, to their people in weekly staff meetings as part of a team development exercise. Some would email them to members of their department over the course of several months. Others would post them next to their monitors as a weekly reminder. One executive team in Asia used them so much that they memorized the numbers of each gem. During their team meetings, members merely mentioned the number of the gem to make a point, and the others understood.

A few of the gems originated with me. The rest came from a variety of sources. I may have been in a meeting, reading a book, watching a movie, overhearing a conversation, or teaching a session with a colleague, when a phrase struck me. Naturally, I wrote it down, took it home and added it to my list. In future lectures or speeches I incorporated it into my teaching—referring to it as a "gem."

I often used these gems as part of my one-on-one coaching sessions with executives. I assigned them to learn, think about, and apply a specific gem that helped them in a targeted area for development. They often posted the gem on their bathroom mirror, computer monitor, or dashboard as a daily reminder. This helped them remember it and apply it—especially when their tendency was to behave in a manner that was contrary to the advice of the gem.

Many professionals added a few of these gems to their own personal philosophy of management, to describe a value or belief in working with others, training team members, or relating to customers and suppliers.

And, of course, the gems were often taken home to help people in their family lives. The application is clearly not just for work. Most of these gems deal with all aspects of one's life—personally, professionally, and organizationally.

Over the years, I started to put the gems in writing so they could be used independent of my teaching. In this collection, you will find each gem, along with an explanation of its basic meaning, application in life situations, and a final section for reflection and self-assessment. I hope you enjoy them, and I encourage you to apply them in your journey toward a more effective and rewarding career and life.

John Parker Stewart

Lake Oswego, Oregon USA

February, 2012

Introduction to the 21 Leadership Dimensions

Over the past 30 years, I have developed and maintained an extensive database built on the results of my feedback assessments from organizations in a variety of industries and government agencies including NASA, U.S. Department of Energy, U.S. Department of Agriculture, telecommunications, government contractors, manufacturers, retail, banking, services, electronics, petroleum, and many others. This assessment has been administered to over 10,000 supervisors, managers, directors, senior executives, presidents and CEOs.

Our feedback instrument (called "360 Personal Feedback Assessment") measures the individual's management performance across 21 leadership dimensions. As shown on next page, the dimensions are organized into four natural groups based on our *LEAD NOW!* leadership model's four quadrants.

LEAD NOW! MODEL
21 Leadership Dimensions

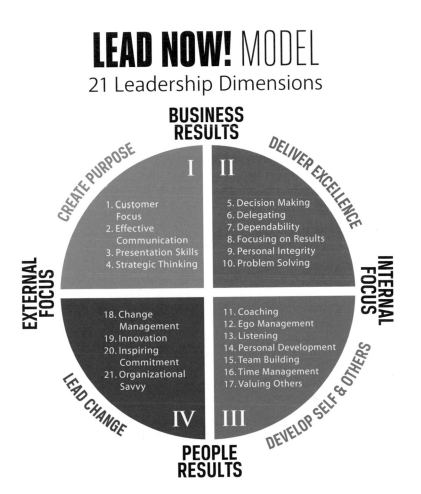

BUSINESS RESULTS

CREATE PURPOSE

DELIVER EXCELLENCE

I
1. Customer Focus
2. Effective Communication
3. Presentation Skills
4. Strategic Thinking

II
5. Decision Making
6. Delegating
7. Dependability
8. Focusing on Results
9. Personal Integrity
10. Problem Solving

EXTERNAL FOCUS

INTERNAL FOCUS

18. Change Management
19. Innovation
20. Inspiring Commitment
21. Organizational Savvy

11. Coaching
12. Ego Management
13. Listening
14. Personal Development
15. Team Building
16. Time Management
17. Valuing Others

LEAD CHANGE

DEVELOP SELF & OTHERS

IV   **III**

PEOPLE RESULTS

Quadrant I: Create Purpose
(Externally Focused Business Results)

A leader is responsible for defining the group's vision and strategy. Creating Purpose identifies what the organization stands for, what it is going to do, and how it is positioned in the marketplace. This involves studying the competition, thoroughly knowing the customer, analyzing industry trends, setting strategy, and communicating effectively to others.

Quadrant II: Deliver Excellence

(Internally Focused Business Results)

A leader is responsible for delivering operational excellence—translating the strategy into day-to-day execution for the organization. This involves clear decision-making, the ability to build consistent and measurable processes, continuous improvement, and behaving with integrity.

Quadrant III: Develop Self & Others

(Internally Focused People Results)

A leader must value learning for him/herself and for others. This involves seeking personal improvement opportunities, building and managing team dynamics, honing technical expertise, managing one's time, coaching and developing others, and managing one's ego.

Quadrant IV: Lead Change

(Externally Focused People Results)

A leader is responsible for creating and championing change efforts that will benefit the organization. This involves influencing key decision makers, sponsoring change projects, empowering stakeholders, encouraging innovation, managing resistance, and making change stick.

Quadrant I: Create Purpose

1. Customer Focus
2. Effective Communication
3. Presentation Skills
4. Strategic Thinking

Quadrant II: Deliver Excellence

5. Decision Making
6. Delegating
7. Dependability
8. Focusing on Results
9. Personal Integrity
10. Problem Solving

Quadrant III: Develop Self & Others

11. Coaching
12. Ego Management
13. Listening
14. Personal Development
15. Team Building
16. Time Management
17. Valuing Others

Quadrant IV: Lead Change

18. Change Management
19. Innovation
20. Inspiring Commitment
21. Organizational Savvy

To help you develop your own leadership capabilities, at the beginning of each chapter, each *Leadership Gem* is referenced to applicable Leadership Dimensions and color coded to the applicable quadrant in the LEAD NOW! model. You can focus on the particular *Gem* that will be the most helpful to your individual development needs. For example, if you need specific help in "Delegating" or "Innovation," you can pay particular attention to those *Gems* that apply to those Dimensions.

We have also provided an Index that lists all of the *52 Gems* in this volume by Leadership Dimension. You will be able to quickly find the *Gem* that fits any of the 21 Leadership Dimensions.

As an additional resource for your personal leadership growth, we recommend that you reference *LEAD NOW! A Personal Leadership Coaching Guide for Results-Driven Leaders* (2012), by John Parker Stewart and Daniel J. Stewart.

52 Leadership Gems

Gem #1

It's amazing what can be accomplished if you don't care who gets the credit.

Related Leadership Dimensions*:

Delegating
Focusing on Results
Ego Management
Team Building
Valuing Others

Color coded to the applicable quadrant in the LEAD NOW! model on page xxiii.

Overview

The need for personal recognition can often become a major stumbling block to team success. Unfortunately, this becomes a major obstacle to team motivation. Ego, unrestrained, has a voracious appetite and paralyzes synergy. Energy applied toward personal recognition becomes a lost commodity.

For example, managers who seek all the glory and accolades can become resented by the team. Success is more likely to occur when the focus is placed on team outcome and not individual performance.

However, when effort and goals are directed toward a *united* purpose, and individuals sacrifice personal recognition for the team's performance, shared objectives are achieved exponentially.

Application

Learn to direct the energy you normally use to advance your own agenda toward building on the combined talents and ideas of those under your leadership.

You will not only create a higher quality result, but you will also be pleasantly surprised at the increased level of motivation among every member of your team. Look for opportunities to give sincere verbal or written credit and appreciation. Use "we" more than "I" in discussions, meetings, and presentations.

Accept responsibility for personal mistakes. Readily acknowledge the ideas of others. Share the spotlight. Go out of your way to recognize others and the role they play. Keep your ego under control. You will be pleased and amazed at the final result, and so will your team!

Reflection

1. To what degree do you seek success and recognition for yourself vs. for your team?

2. How often do you take advantage of opportunities to sincerely praise others?

3. When you are singled out for special recognition by those in authority, do you look for ways to express how others helped you and include them in the recognition?

4. Look back over your past successes. Honestly consider how much the help you received from others contributed to those successes.

5. Identify times and ways you can "catch" others doing something well.

Gem #2

An action deferred
is a tension
retained.

Related Leadership Dimensions:

Dependability

Focusing on Results

Time Management

Overview

Years ago there was a variety show on television where one of the most popular acts involved a man who balanced spinning plates on top of long thin poles. The audience was fascinated that he was able to constantly run back and forth across the stage keeping the plates spinning. Amazingly, not one plate ever crashed to the floor. But such a stressful balancing act could only last for a short time.

Professionals of all varieties find themselves in a similar situation—balancing all kinds of tasks they must juggle in a typical day. They have to make sure that not one task slips and falls. Everyone is counting on them. These responsibilities are heavy and demanding. Most days are filled with to-do lists that must be done: assignments, requests, and action items from colleagues, supervisors, family, and friends. Each time an item on the list is deferred, it creates tension—the same tension and stress of another spinning plate. Consequently, the sooner a task is addressed, the sooner the tension is reduced or even eliminated.

Application

Think of all that is thrown at you during any given day. You are the willing or unwilling recipient of countless actions from work, home, school, and the community. It can be overwhelming to process and complete all of these tasks, especially when you procrastinate or don't prioritize.

Look at how you manage your assignments. Items that are frequently put off until tomorrow begin to add up, creating overwhelming to-do lists in the future. The more tasks that are deferred, the greater the stress you will experience. Begin to take action on issues right away or as soon as possible. Don't delay. Take action!

Even for large problems, taking the first step will decrease anxiety and enable you to better prioritize all of the other items (or plates) you are juggling. As a result, you will be amazed at the amount of tension that will disappear—allowing you to breathe again.

Reflection

1. How do you manage your own stress level?

2. Honestly consider how much stress and tension is added to your load as a result of un-done tasks.

3. Consider what causes you to procrastinate. Are you waiting for a *chunk* of time before tackling a large task? Are you hoping that conditions will change? Is the task unpleasant? Once you learn why you tend to procrastinate, determine how you can overcome these barriers.

4. When learning of new tasks, first ask yourself: "What can be delegated?"

5. Consider the specific cost of procrastination in *your* job. Moving ahead on small, nagging tasks will free your mind for more important *thinking* issues your job requires.

Gem #3

We judge ourselves by our intentions. Others judge us by our actions.

Related Leadership Dimensions:

Customer Focus
Personal Integrity
Coaching
Personal Development
Change Management

Overview

The majority of leaders have good intentions. They want to succeed, they want to deliver results, and they want their people to be engaged and satisfied.

While these might be their intentions, their actions often tell a different story. The intensity of their schedules and pressures often nullify many of these good intentions. These actions include not communicating regularly with peers, not developing their direct reports, not championing change efforts, and not keeping a pulse on the culture of the organization. To the leaders, it is an unintentional oversight or something they intend to address in the future. But to the person on the neglected end, it seems intentional and it is not forgotten.

Leaders evaluate themselves by their intentions, but their people only have observable actions to remember and interpret. This results in different perceptions that can diminish their followers' commitment and attitude.

Application

Create a list of what you wanted to do last week and what you actually did. Then identify how others might interpret your *actions*, not your *intentions*. Ask a trusted peer to validate these interpretations. This will provide insight into how others see you.

With this information, you can now craft a plan to correct misperceptions. Begin with identifying how you would like others to perceive you. Then be specific about what behaviors can create that perception and what behaviors could derail this effort. With this action plan, you can better align your intentions to reality, moving from good intentions to meaningful actions.

Your people will begin to see you as authentic and transparent, and their respect for you will increase. The bottom line is you will become more effective in your ability to lead, and consequently your people will be more committed to you. Your intentions will match your actions.

Reflection

1. The first step to applying this gem is to take advantage of small and frequent "5-minute" moments during your day to address your intentions.

2. Take a moment and think of some of your best intentions over the past few months—for example, thanking an employee for her help on a project, congratulating a teammate on his success, explaining the rationale for a decision, and visit with employees in their work space.

3. Once you have listed some of your intentions, note how many of them actually happened. Are there intentions that did not turn into actions?

4. What stopped you from following through with your intentions?

5. What could you do differently in the future to ensure that your good intentions become actions?

Gem #4

The biggest hurdle to effective communication is the assumption that it has taken place.

Related Leadership Dimensions:

Effective Communication

Presentation Skills

Delegating

Listening

Inspiring Commitment

Overview

Communication is at the heart of all relationships, projects and activities. Yet, no matter how hard we try, we often wonder why there is a communication breakdown when our message seemed so clear at the time. How can individuals emerge from the same meeting hearing the same words, but have varied levels of understanding or interpretation? For example, a leader spends all morning in a meeting putting forth excessive effort to clarify every detail on a major team project, only to learn that many attending the meeting were completely confused.

A false assumption in communication is believing that everyone in the loop has received and understood the message. Leaders must remember that others have a different perspective, which may distort the intended meaning.

Leaders must accept as a constant that when two or more minds attempt to communicate, they are coming from at least two different perspectives. With this awareness, communication becomes a process that requires greater clarification and ongoing monitoring.

Application

Accept that the need for clarifying questions and responses is a routine part of communication—even though it will require extra time and effort. Your investment will reap major dividends. This alone will help reduce frustration and minimize misunderstandings. You will also save time by not having to resolve these unfortunate and time-consuming situations.

At the conclusion of an important conversation or meeting, avoid generalities such as "Do you have any questions?" People often do not ask questions because they may not want to draw attention to themselves in front of others or they may be so confused they don't know what to ask. Instead, try asking them clarifying questions that require a response such as: "What is your understanding of our approach?" or "What are your next steps in the project?"

Their answers will help you see where additional emphasis or information is needed. Actively seek clarification to your communications to avoid misunderstandings.

Reflection

1. Realize that everybody—CEOs, presidents, middle managers, employees, teachers, mechanics, lawyers, doctors, politicians, parents, ministers, coaches, actors, students—*all* have trouble communicating. It's a lifelong challenge!

2. We frequently do not have all the necessary information so we end up making assumptions and regarding them as fact. Honestly consider how often you do this.

3. Don't ever assume you have successfully communicated—especially on important issues. Regularly check to see if your message was received, and if it was received as you intended.

4. In a group meeting where assignments are made, as the leader, verify if everyone is on track by asking questions. If they are unsure, take the time to clarify and ensure that there is understanding.

5. In communicating, keep in mind that each person is unique. How can you take that into account when preparing for and engaging in communication?

Gem #5

A problem well defined is a problem half-solved.

-Peter Drucker

Related Leadership Dimensions:

Strategic Thinking
Decision Making
Focusing on Results
Problem Solving

Overview

Peter Drucker is considered the father of modern management theory. During his life, he was often asked to help organizations facing overwhelming problems.

When I studied under him, he told me that upon his arrival at a client's location, the corporate leaders would greet him and proceed to tell him *their* view of the problem. He listened and then replied, "No, that's not the problem." This frustrated them. He then explained that they were only seeing symptoms of the real problem, not the actual problem. They needed to dig deeper. Frustrated, they tried again, to which he typically replied that they were still only looking at the symptoms.

After a few hours of this back and forth process, they finally stopped addressing symptoms and figured out how to focus on defining the *root* problem. Once the actual problem was properly defined, he would tell them how vital it is to *first* carefully and accurately define the real problem. Only at that stage of the process could they truly begin to solve the problem, AND it was now half-solved.

Application

No doubt, you and your team have struggled with solving large, overwhelming problems. They may have been related to marketing, people, budget, quality control, logistics, or a myriad of organizational issues.

Don't be deceived by defining a problem based upon initial appearances or convenient data. Remember Peter Drucker's sage advice: ask yourself if you have properly defined the problem. Make sure your definition of the problem doesn't just address symptoms of the real issue. Be sure your problem statement is relevant to the deeper concern and that it is not merely ancillary to the root cause. Determine if you have found what Drucker called "an elephant," meaning the group has identified an overwhelming problem that is too big to address and must be broken down into smaller parts before it can be solved.

The process of considering these aspects of problem solving is time consuming and frustrating, but well worth it once you have defined the actual problem *correctly* and *clearly*. And once your problem is properly defined, you are already half-way to the solution!

Reflection

1. Are you able to distinguish between the root problem and the symptom(s) of the problem? How?

2. Do you sometimes define your problem too broadly and inclusively—making it what Peter Drucker would call an "elephant"? If so, how can you make that elephant "bite sized"? If you can't break it down into manageable chunks, you will likely be unsuccessful in resolving it.

3. Are you too close to the problem to see and understand it properly? If so, what outside help can you seek to provide a fresh, objective perspective?

4. Identify techniques you could use to help your entire team stay focused on uncovering and defining the root problem. Dr. Drucker recommended the use of whiteboards or flip charts rather than individual note-taking because this promotes mutually shared visual focus.

5. When the process seems laborious or discouraging, remember the value of a properly defined problem—when this is done, you're problem is half-solved!

Gem #6

27 years of
genuine growth or
1 year repeated
27 times?

Related Leadership Dimensions:

Focusing on Results
Coaching
Ego Management
Personal Development

Overview

During initial executive coaching sessions, I often ask the people I am coaching how many years of professional experience they bring to the table. Their response is revealing. The answers usually vary, but are often stated with pride and even arrogance: something like, "I have been working for 27 years!"

Upon hearing the response, I wonder to myself, "Hmmm . . . does this person mean 27 years of cumulative experience OR 1 year of learning repeated 27 times?" There is a world of difference between these two scenarios. The first yields progress, learning, advancement, vitality, and vigor. The other yields stagnation and paralysis—demonstrating little if any growth.

Strong leaders seek new opportunities to continually develop and adapt their people skills and strategy skills year after year. Poor leaders gather a few tools and ideas early in their careers, and then struggle, in futility and frustration, to make limited and out-of-date knowledge and skills apply to the challenges of a dynamic and complex world. Like compounded interest, strong leaders take advantage of every opportunity to grow and take their skills to a higher level.

Application

Your working years can speed by as you attend meetings, manage projects, meet deadlines, refine budgets, help and guide employees, receive promotions, and face challenges. With all that *busyness*, it is difficult for a professional to find time to learn, progress, and sharpen needed skills in a demanding and competitive world. It takes discipline and desire to find the time to study and grow.

For example, over the course of coaching countless professionals, I have seen several who have had little or no interest in growing their level of skill or knowledge. They do not make personal study and improvement a priority. And their performance, or lack of it, clearly shows it.

Be careful of merely repeating years over the course of your career. Make each additional year in your work one of genuine learning and growth. Look at your capacity for better people skills, interpersonal awareness, technical competency, leadership capability, and business acumen. Make sure they are improving each year. Compounded growth produces productive and high-quality leaders.

Reflection

1. Do you read leadership and management books? When was the last time you enrolled in a class or seminar on management and people skills, such as innovation, strategy, or listening?

2. Is there a possibility that you were promoted into management because you did a great job as a technical contributor? If so, do you find yourself ill-prepared for leadership roles? How can you adapt to your new role?

3. How openly do you view the results of a self-assessment instrument, a 360 feedback survey, or any type of feedback from your people? (This can be a big eye-opener.)

4. How are you *really* doing? Do you seek input from your people on your leadership effectiveness? Do you act on the results?

5. Being brutally honest, ask yourself what your attitude is on learning and trying to improve in your overall professional development. Do you learn from mistakes? Do you stay on top of your game? Do you stretch yourself in new areas?

Gem #7

Four magic words: "What do you think?"

Related Leadership Dimensions:

Decision Making

Team Building

Valuing Others

Change Management

Inspiring Commitment

Overview

L eaders often assume they have the right answer. They may go into a meeting or small group discussion believing they already know the solution or appropriate steps to take. Consequently, they will feel little need to genuinely seek the views of others. Their people can sense this and will feel undervalued. Overusing this *"leader-is-always-right"* approach can prevent critical insights and alternative suggestions from others.

On the other hand, starting a meeting or conversation with these four magic words: "what do you think?" can foster richer dialogue, deeper employee engagement, a strong sense of ownership, feeling valued, and better decisions.

When these four words are used, team members will feel a greater sense of buy-in, inclusion, and appreciation. The leader will consequently better leverage the team's talents, experience and expertise resulting in genuine *synergy* to reach high quality decisions, actions and solutions.

Application

During a given day, tally how many times you ask others what they think. The total might surprise you. Set a goal to improve this behavior with your team and/or with each employee by using these magic words more often. Commit to increasing the frequency that you ask these four words.

This simple phrase will also remind you that a leader does not need to have all the answers. Using these four inclusive words is evidence of an effective and healthy leader who actively listens to the input of the members of the team. Your people will feel valued by you because you asked them for their opinion, demonstrating that you care about what they think.

That act alone can do more toward earning their hearts than anything else. They will feel included, needed, and important because their leader asked for their opinion. This magical, open-ended question will build a stronger sense of ownership in the team and greater camaraderie among the members. And your leadership will be stronger and more effective.

Reflection

1. How do you feel when your opinion is sincerely sought? What difference does it make in your attitude, your commitment, and your loyalty to the person who asked you?

2. How often do you enter a meeting with a pre-determined solution in mind? Be open to the input of others as you make a final decision.

3. What steps can you take to ensure that your "problem solving meetings" *genuinely* include your people? They will know if these meetings are a charade.

4. Try an experiment: use these four words often and watch the result in the faces of your team members. Notice how it impacts their attitudes, willingness to contribute, and their sense of being appreciated.

5. Take the time to list some ways, times, and places when you can ask "what do you think?" Identify who you should ask, as well as how and when. You'll be amazed how easy it becomes, not to mention what you learn.

Gem #8

People tend
to support
what they help
create.

Related Leadership Dimensions:

Decision Making
Valuing Others
Change Management
Inspiring Commitment

Overview

Creation is a pervasive human instinct. We enjoy the chance to create something—whether it is a piece of art, a new floor plan, a delicious meal, a book club, a garden, a program, a strategic overview, or a solution to a nagging problem. Rendering, drafting, creating—these are common drives in all of us.

So it makes sense that we naturally prefer to participate in programs, groups, and even procedures that we helped create. It is also typical to feel some resentment toward decisions, policies, demands, changes, and programs that are imposed on us without our input, especially when the "new way" affects us directly. But when we are invited to provide ideas on such matters, our willingness to support the result increases.

When leaders choose to include their people in the process of making decisions, shaping policies, and adopting programs, they are acknowledging people's innate drive to contribute and to feel a greater part of it. As a result, they will reward their leader with increased effort, trust, and support.

Application

Recall recent decisions that you have made that affected your team and the extent to which you included them in the decision-making process. Contrast this with your people's reactions to decisions and policies they did not help create or participate in.

When decisions are made without creative input from the people affected by those decisions and policies, they may respond with outward acceptance—lip service—but never fully support the decision or policy. This reaction from your people is detrimental to the success of individual decisions and the team's work as a whole.

You need your team's support on decisions that will be made. This will likely happen if they are part of the process. Include them in decision-making. Present the options and seek their opinions. Share the relevant background information and let them be part of the solution. You will be pleasantly surprised by the support they will tend to give the final decision—all because you included them.

Reflection

1. How do you feel and react when a significant decision that impacts you is made without your input? Your people will likely feel the same way.

2. Are you willing to ask your boss for more time to make a decision in order to seek the opinions of those who work with you who will be affected by the decision?

3. Identify ways that you can increase input from your team members when decisions are made, policies are changed, or new programs developed.

4. How can you involve your people in the decision-making process even when you are already certain of what the decision needs to be?

5. If early participation in the decision-making process is not possible, identify alternative ways you can help your team to be included in the change process.

Gem #9

If you don't take care of your customer, someone else will.

Related Leadership Dimensions:

Customer Focus
Dependability
Focusing on Results
Listening
Organizational Savvy

Overview

Today's customers are well-informed, share information with each other, and research products. Their needs are never-ending. These buyers seem to always want something better, faster, and cheaper. They also want to be treated with consistency, courtesy, and respect.

There seems to be no end to the alternative vendors that customers can select. What this really means is that their last interaction with your company could be just that—the last time they buy from you. If you don't take care of them during each phase of the transaction, there are plenty of other companies and vendors waiting to meet their needs. And they will easily and speedily find one to replace you.

You aren't the only one in the game. The marketplace is full of vendors waiting in line, nipping at your heels, strategizing to win over your customers. Take care of your customers or someone else will.

Application

Identify who your customers are as well as their current and future needs. Rank these needs as high, medium, or low. Assess your current customer service practices to see how they address the high and medium customer needs you've identified. Then ask yourself what needs to be changed.

Your current policies and behaviors should provide a satisfying customer experience every time. Ask your customers what kind of experience they are having. As a leader, focus your daily conversations around the identified customer needs and develop metrics to measure your performance as well as their satisfaction. Stay in touch with them. Remain aware of your customers' changing tastes and wants.

Too many businesses become complacent, aloof, and arrogant toward their customers, and consequently, their customers take their business elsewhere. The above techniques will help you stay close to your customers and respond to their needs and tastes so they will continue to *choose you* instead of your competition.

Reflection

1. How do you stay in touch with the whims and changing tastes of your customers? Do your methods really work? (Don't kid yourself.)

2. What techniques are your competitors using? How successful are they in gathering accurate data?

3. What percentage of your time do you spend discussing and analyzing your customer? Do you have an accurate feel for a typical "customer experience" with your business?

4. How do you solicit customer feedback? Is it reliable and valid? Does it provide what you need to know? Are you sure?

5. When you learn of customer concerns or frustrations, how do you respond? Is your response swift, satisfying, and fair? Your customers talk to each other; what message do you want them to share?

Gem #10

Ask yourself: "What is it like to work for me?"

Related Leadership Dimensions:

Coaching
Ego Management
Personal Development
Valuing Others
Inspiring Commitment

Overview

It is easy for leaders to view things solely from their own point of view. It is an automatic and natural way of evaluating their own leadership ability. However, that one-sided (and biased) view can be very misleading. It can lead to major blind spots that prevent leaders from seeing serious flaws in their own skills and competencies.

All leaders must come to understand the vital importance of seeking other points of view regarding their own leadership. Feedback from others is often the only means for leaders to accurately assess their capabilities and opportunities.

Asking the difficult but revealing question: "What is it like to work for me?" will push leaders outside of their own mental framework and help them consider how others perceive them. The perceptions of the leader's people are the ones that matter most.

Application

Too often, well-intentioned, highly capable leaders operate in partial darkness. Their self-awareness is blinded because they do not have accurate and current perceptions of their own leadership. Think of leaders who rely solely on their own perception in how they manage daily challenges. These blind spots will eventually catch up with them—sadly after it is too late.

This lack of awareness cripples an otherwise talented leader. If you believe you display strong leadership qualities, but others disagree, seriously consider their point of view. Solicit clarification. Take advantage of objective assessments. Seek honest, non-threatening feedback.

Spend time imagining yourself in your people's shoes. Picture yourself in a meeting or in an informal conversation. View the encounter through their eyes. What behaviors do you see? What messages are your behaviors sending? Are these the messages you want others to receive? If not, it is time to change your leadership behavior by applying this Leadership Gem.

Reflection

1. When was the last time you had a formalized assessment?

2. Are you aware of your strengths and areas that need improvement? Has your perception been validated by others?

3. Do you genuinely invite and welcome feedback from others regarding desirable skills and talents as well as your liabilities?

4. When others wish to share with you their point of view of how you could be more effective, are you approachable, and non-defensive? (This sends a powerful signal to them!)

5. How do you initially react when you learn of areas you need to address? Do you justify or rationalize? Or do you try to understand and apply the feedback to improve and fully address appropriate and needed changes?

Gem #11

When you're
green you grow.
When you're ripe
you rot.

Related Leadership Dimensions:

Focusing on Results
Ego Management
Personal Development
Change Management
Innovation

Overview

Ionce had an apple tree in the back yard. Every spring, the buds on the tree limbs would open up revealing flowers. Soon these flowers were replaced by small, young apples. During the summer, the green apples received the sunlight, water, and nutrients to grow and develop. As fall came, the apples turned red, became ripe, and stopped growing.

The ripe apples that we did not pick fell off the tree and began to rot on the ground. These once young and growing apples were now old, decaying fruit. No one wanted them anymore. They were of no use to anyone.

Apples grow the most when they are green. "Green" is a word often used to describe a new employee. While more tenured professionals use the term as something of an insult, being green is a great benefit. When we are new and green, like the apple, we recognize our need to learn and grow. If we become too complacent in our jobs, we stop growing and "rot" professionally. It all boils down to one's attitude toward learning, growing and improving.

Application

New or "green" leaders are often open to different ideas and possibilities. They are interested in learning from others and improving their ability to perform the varied aspects of their job. They see things in a different light. They often want to prepare for the next position that has increased responsibilities.

Unfortunately, leaders sometimes reach a point where they are less concerned about their own personal development. As this happens, they gradually change from green to ripe. While mature leaders are needed, they can rot and perish if they do not continue to learn, grow, and progress.

Consider the degree to which you approach situations. Do you have an eager desire to learn, or do you have a resistance to learning? Analyze what you read, study, and expose your mind to. Take advantage of opportunities in which you will learn new trends, techniques, and methods. Look for ways to improve any aspect of your capabilities and skills. Stay fresh and green. Like good fresh apples, you will be in high demand.

Reflection

1. What is your honest attitude toward learning—beyond the minimal job requirements?

2. How do you spend your free time? Do you focus on exercising your mind as well as your body?

3. What do you read in your down time: professional journals, novels, self-help books, texts, histories, and biographies?

4. Do you occasionally attend classes, seminars, training sessions, lectures, and discussions?

5. Do you believe that if you read, study, and learn more, you would be better prepared to handle greater job responsibilities? Try it; you have nothing to lose and everything to gain.

Gem #12

Listen with your ears AND your eyes.

Related Leadership Dimensions:

Customer Focus
Effective Communication
Listening
Valuing Others
Inspiring Commitment

Overview

As small children we were taught to open our ears when we listened. Listening with our ears comes naturally to us, but most of us haven't considered or learned the bigger part of effective listening—listening with our eyes.

Research findings reveal that about 80 percent or more of all communication is non-verbal. Only 20 percent consists of the spoken word. Yet look at all the emphasis that is placed on the latter.

What this really means is that if you listen only with your ears, you will miss the large majority of a message. Well-trained eyes will tune in to nonverbal signals. Nonverbal communication includes facial cues, body language, outward appearances, clothing, and emotions such as anger, frustration, happiness, surprise, and hurt.

The inability to see and understand these signals can significantly diminish a leader's ability to understand others. This directly hinders effective communication, not to mention relationships and people skills.

Application

The human brain can process data far faster than the average person speaks. As a result, the mind can easily wander when one is listening. We all know what a temptation it is to let our minds go off to another thought while we should be paying attention to our boss, friend or family member who is speaking to us. It takes practice and discipline to focus on improving your interpersonal communication.

Consider how you listen and what you focus on during conversations? Don't just take in the words through your ears. Pay close attention to the large number of nonverbal cues emitted by the speaker. This all requires attentive discipline to prevent the mind from wandering. To truly catch the entire message in the communication, engage both your ears *and* your eyes as you concentrate on the intended meaning of the message.

Doing so will greatly improve your understanding and overall listening capabilities—dramatically enhancing your people skills and *your success*.

Reflection

1. How aware are you of the weight and influence that non-verbal communication has in overall communication?

2. How much of your listening behavior involves your eyes instead of just your ears?

3. When you listen, do you find that you are concentrating so hard on getting your point across that you are not aware of the listener's reaction to you? Focusing on non-verbal signals will enhance your awareness.

4. Do you discover that your driving priority is waiting for the other person to pause—so that you can quickly interject your point? If so, you are likely missing the bulk of their message.

5. Think of varied techniques you could use to remind you to *watch* more as you listen. For instance, you could keep your eyes focused on their face as you have a conversation; their eyes and facial expressions are very revealing.

Gem #13

People only care how much you know, when they know how much you care.

Related Leadership Dimensions:

Coaching
Valuing Others
Change Management
Inspiring Commitment
Organizational Savvy

Overview

Several years ago, I learned of a high ranking government official who had years of public experience and was highly skilled at maneuvering through the legislative process. Despite all of his expertise, his colleagues purposely avoided him and intentionally worked against his proposals and initiatives for no other reason than that they were *his* ideas. His reputation among his associates was toxic.

The reason for this was simply that he failed to show any interest in others. He did not ask their opinion. He dominated conversations. He never showed that he cared about anyone else, because he didn't. His ego was out of control. He felt the world rotated around him. What a tragedy to see such intelligence and expertise wasted because he didn't care about anyone else. In truth, he was very bright and had many talents, yet he had these fatal flaws.

Even worse was the way he made others feel because of his demeaning attitude toward them. As a result, nobody cared about him, his ideas, his efforts, or his future. In fact, the reverse was true: they rejoiced in his failures.

Application

There are many behaviors you can employ to let your people know you sincerely care about them. As an example, consider a recent conversation you've had with a colleague or employee. If you asked for their ideas, honestly listened to what they had to say, and then paused to consider their comments, you sent a powerful message about how much you care about them.

Having expertise or knowledge is not always sufficient in encouraging someone to listen to you. Unless you first help your employees feel valued, they may not hear anything you say. Over the next week, identify and practice one listening tip or behavior. For example, you could ask open-ended questions and genuinely listen to their reply, instead of mentally preparing your response while they are still expressing their views. At the end of the week, assess the overall responses you received from others.

In addition to improved listening skills, there are ways that you can let others feel you value and care about them, such as including them in decisions that affect them or showing interest in their personal lives. People will care more about what you need or want them to do once they know you genuinely care about them.

Reflection

1. Consider how much you think the following things impact your people's attitude and performance: your educational degrees, your title, your salary, your years of experience, and your ideas. These things may mean more to you than to the team.

2. What are some of the ways you can let your teammates, colleagues, employees, and family members know you care about them?

3. Since the use of good listening skills is one of the most effective methods you can use to show others that you value them, what can you do to improve your listening skills? What can you do more of or less of?

4. Do you include others in decisions that will affect them? Do you acknowledge others' ideas and contributions above your own? Get out of your own thoughts and open up to theirs.

5. How aware are you of the off-the-job aspects of your team members' lives, such as family, hobbies, vacation plans, and classes they are taking?

Gem #14

In the decision-making process, voice your opinion last!

Related Leadership Dimensions:

Effective Communication

Decision Making

Problem Solving

Valuing Others

Change Management

Overview

Upon studying the process President John F. Kennedy used as he struggled to solve the volatile Cuban Missile Crisis in the early 1960s, we learn that during the deliberations with his national security team, President Kennedy never voiced his own opinion on what he thought should be done. Nobody on his team knew what the president was thinking—not even his brother and confidant, Bobby Kennedy, the Attorney General.

Only after three tense days, at the end of the debate, did he finally express his own views. Of course, his original opinion had now been refined by the team's recommendations. Gratefully, the correct course of action was taken and nuclear war with the Soviet Union was avoided.

President Kennedy knew that if leaders express their views early in a team's discussion, it will bias the group and prevent other, perhaps better, solutions from being considered. The leader's opinion has strong influence over others and will usually sway and stifle inputs, quality, innovation, and decisions.

Application

Recognize the value of involving your team in critical decisions, especially decisions that will affect them. The effectiveness of these discussions depends on the free flow of their creative and innovative perspectives while you, the leader, keep your opinions to yourself so others are not biased by your view.

Be careful not to express your views either *verbally* or *nonverbally*. Be aware that your people will watch your face and mannerisms as they respond with their inputs. Encourage their ideas during the discussion so that all their thoughts and suggestions are expressed. During your team sessions, actively encourage their participation in the discussion. Solicit their input. Smile and nod as they express their views. Put them at ease so their ideas flow. Encourage comfortable and open dialogue.

Then, at the end, you will likely see how the quality and creativity of the discussion contributed to a better solution than what you would have made by yourself. This way you and your team will experience the benefit of true synergy!

Reflection

1. Think back over recent decision-making experiences with your team. When did you express your opinion—in the early stages, in the middle, toward the end, or not all?

2. When you do express your views early, note how often the inputs of your team mirror the views you have just expressed. This demonstrates how their thoughts will be biased by your opinion because of your position.

3. Your role as the leader is very influential to your team. Identify ways you can encourage your teammates to speak freely and openly. Your constant encouragement is essential. Never put them or their ideas down.

4. What specific methods do you use to encourage your team to express their ideas and suggestions freely?

5. How can you create a brainstorming atmosphere where no idea is eliminated or critiqued in the early stages— especially by the leader?

Gem #15

Ownership
or
rentership.

Related Leadership Dimensions:
Dependability
Focusing on Results
Coaching
Team Building
Inspiring Commitment

Overview

We have likely all been renters at some point in our lives. The apartment where we lived belonged to the landlord. Usually, its care and maintenance were not high on our list of priorities. If something went wrong, was damaged, torn or chipped it was the landlord's problem—not ours.

But then, the day arrived where we had saved enough money to qualify for our *own* mortgage on our *own* house. Now we had an entirely new attitude toward the property. We were quick to notice when something was not functioning properly. We took care of the wiring and the plumbing. We tried not to scratch the walls and fixtures. We avoided spills on the carpet. We felt great pride in it because it was *our house*!

This analogy applies to the attitude our people have in an organization. They can view themselves as merely renters or as owners. Their choice makes a huge difference in their attitude and performance. The leader has a major influence on which one they choose.

Application

Each of these two attitudes represents entirely different mindsets—and each leads to a major disparity in their respective levels of motivation. The *renter* mentality is detached and involves little commitment. The *owner* mentality is constant and committed.

Your people all see themselves as either renters or owners within your organization. Think of the level of commitment they have to your organization and its goals, customers, standards, services, growth, quality, and reputation. How your people view their relationship to you and your company will determine their attitude. Of all the factors that contribute to your people's attitude, your behavior toward them is the single most important influence.

When you choose to involve your people in decisions that affect them, they will feel valued because they know their opinions matter. They will also be far more inclined to support the final decision because they feel a sense of ownership. Your people can feel like renters or owners. The choice is yours.

Reflection

1. Recall when you rented something like an apartment, a moving truck, or a rental car. How committed were you to its care compared to when you are the owner?

2. Do you treat your people as if you are the landlord and they are the tenants?

3. What parallels exist between the "renter vs. owner" attitude and an employee's commitment level to an employer?

4. Identify the behaviors that your supervisor or manager engages in which impact your attitude toward your company. Determine ways you can use positive practices with your people.

5. To what extent do you include, involve, and engage your people in decisions and problem-solving? Can you see the difference this will make in their attitude and commitment?

Gem #16

Beware the "#1 Syndrome".

Related Leadership Dimensions:

Customer Focus

Strategic Thinking

Focusing on Results

Ego Management

Organizational Savvy

Overview

A very successful coach said that his biggest fear for his team was to be identified number one in the pre-season rankings. He cited two reasons for his concern. First, he was afraid his players would start to believe it. Second, he knew his team would become a target—every other team would try their hardest to knock his team out of that top position.

An historical look at many industries reveals that the market share leader often does not last long, for similar reasons. A careful study of many industries reveals that companies in the lead position usually slipped from their dominance in a relatively short time. Being considered first in your team, department, company, or industry in terms of performance or market share is admirable.

However, the danger is allowing yourself to become complacent. Over time, the dreaded attitudes of complacency, arrogance, and invulnerability creep into your thinking. Once the air of superiority prevails, while the competitors become stronger, your inevitable decline or fall is soon to follow.

Application

In the rental car business in the 1970s, the CEO of Avis promoted the slogan "We're #2, and we try harder!" It turned out to be very successful for them as they went head to head against #1 Hertz. Having this mindset in your career and your organization is healthy.

Success and market dominance can be fleeting and fickle. Act like you are always fighting to do better. Examine every aspect of your business to see how and where you can improve the quality of your systems, processes, communication, and customer service. Always look for a better way. Seek out and study best practices. Solicit honest feedback from your customers. Stay closely tuned to what your competition is doing. Don't get caught in paradigm ruts, like "we've always done it this way."

Whether or not you are currently #1, adopt the mental slogan, "We try harder." Someone will always be trying to surpass you. Don't let them succeed. If you are the market leader, keep on working like you are #2 so you will remain #1.

Reflection

1. How rigorously do you analyze your competition?
2. How do you keep your own ego in check? A leader's attitude is more contagious than you will ever realize.
3. How do you measure continuous improvement to avoid complacency? Do you analyze your progress frequently and respond appropriately?
4. How effective are your post-project reviews to identify lessons learned?
5. How do you encourage negative and constructive feedback about your organization or yourself? This feedback will help you see more objectively.

Gem #17

"Good is the enemy of great."

—Jim Collins

Related Leadership Dimensions:

Strategic Thinking

Focusing on Results

Personal Development

Team Building

Change Management

Overview

Imagine a company embracing the motto, "We are no worse than anyone else." It sounds silly. However, too often organizations settle for average performance. The attitude seems to be: "Keep up with the competition, we are just as good as they are."

In such an atmosphere, improvement is stifled and even resisted. Change is slow and reactive. Employees are more interested in maintaining the status quo than making waves. Upon examining the consistent market share leaders in any industry, it is apparent that they have developed a culture where every aspect of the business can and should be improved. They have accepted and endorsed the paradigm that there is always a better way.

These are the organizations who rocket to the top in quality, service, repeat business, and customer satisfaction. To them, nothing is good enough. They constantly seek ongoing improvements. Their quality is superior. They have a passion for greatness.

Application

Take an honest look at the attitude you bring to your job. Do you view "good" as good enough? Remember that your philosophy and demeanor are contagious, they speak volumes to others. Those you work with sense how you think, and may copy it, especially if you are in leadership.

Think of the aspects of your job or organization that could go from being merely good to being better and then even great? Imagine if all of your team started to look for ways to improve the way they work, how they perform each aspect of the job, and every skill and phase of leadership. Consider what the result would be if you and your team raised the bar of expectation to a higher level. Visualize the results in terms of productivity, reputation and overall performance.

Do not allow good to be the standard. Introduce *great* into your expectations, and follow through with the commensurate effort. You will be amazed at the results, and you will no longer settle for anything less than *great*!

Reflection

1. Are you objective enough to take a comprehensive reading of your "good enough" pulse? You may need a competent outsider to give you a trusted, objective assessment to help you.

2. When was the last time you thoroughly reviewed each phase of your operation to see how and where it could be improved?

3. Does the notion of "continuous improvement" ring hollow to you—as if it is a faddish cliche? Or do you take its meaning seriously?

4. Imagine the difference it would make if your organization were a few degrees better in each phase of your processes.

5. Where do you stand on the "good to great" spectrum in terms of your own personal development, your professional performance, and your team's performance? How could you move closer to "great" in each category? Ask your team to design a plan that would incrementally help the organization improve. Can you take them to the next level?

Gem #18

No one likes
surprises!

Related Leadership Dimensions:

Customer Focus
Effective Communication
Change Management
Inspiring Commitment

Overview

There are three types of news: 1) good news, 2) bad news, and 3) no news. When people are asked which of the three they prefer, it's no surprise that they respond: "good news." When asked which they prefer the least, the answer is usually: "no news."

This means that people would rather have bad news than be kept in the dark, having to wonder what is happening. In the absence of any news, they will often assume the worst—filling in the unknown with their own thoughts and fears about the circumstance. Even though bad news is disappointing and unpleasant, it prevents the fretting, speculating, and negative assumptions that "no news" brings.

This applies to surprises as well. Surprises catch people off guard and unprepared. Leaders and employees prefer to be kept in the loop—apprised of the latest information so they can be prepared to respond to the many uncertainties of the future. In short, nobody likes surprises, except possibly on a birthday.

Application

Think of the times that key information has been withheld from you. You probably felt upset, overlooked, and disconnected. You were caught off-guard and didn't appreciate it.

Sometimes bad news is held back to prevent a negative reaction; however, once the truth comes out, employees nearly always wish they had known of it earlier. Knowing the bad news helps them prepare an appropriate response and/or make informed decisions.

Diplomacy and timing are important; but whenever possible, avoid delaying the sharing of news (however bad) with your boss, your team, or your customers. This will give them needed time to prepare a mitigation plan or other necessary action. The information might not be pleasant, but it is better than keeping them in the dark. Don't let them get caught unprepared. Be open and inform them of important information. It will build stronger and more trusting relationships. It will improve your leadership and their results.

Reflection

1. How do you feel when you are kept in the dark regarding important changes or emerging conditions? Even when the news is bad, would you rather be kept informed?

2. What do you do to keep people in the loop? When do you share information? If you withhold information, what is your reason? How does it end up making them feel?

3. When you have significant and/or negative news to share with your boss, your team, or your customers, how do you go about delivering the news? Do you tell them in person? Do you send an email? The method you employ makes a big difference in how they react. Select it wisely.

4. How can you improve the way you disseminate information to your people? What should you take into account?

5. Put yourself in the shoes of your people. What would you like to know? What news would you want to be aware of, and when? How would you prefer to receive it? Your answers to these questions will open your eyes to how well you truly know your people.

Gem #19

Swim in *their* tank.

Related Leadership Dimensions:

Ego Management
Listening
Team Building
Valuing Others
Inspiring Commitment

Overview

Killer whale trainers have a specific pattern they follow to earn the trust of these large sea creatures. The process is fascinating and carefully orchestrated based on years of successful experience.

Trainers establish a playful relationship with the whale before they ever get into the water. Then, the trainers get into the whale's tank with the whale. They splash and play together. They swim together. During this time, trainers feed the whale, stroke its mouth and nose, and copy its motions. This interaction can last several months to let the whale know that no harm will come to it.

Over time, this type of behavior by the trainers replaces the whale's natural suspicion with trust toward these strangers in its world. Once the trust and comfort is in place, then the formal training of teaching the whale tricks and performance behaviors begins.

Application

As a leader, you must teach certain skills, ways of thinking, and standards of behavior with your people to help you meet your targets. You can spend your limited resources with time-consuming and expensive training, but none of it will "stick" if you have not first earned the trust of your people.

Not only must you let them know that you mean them no harm, you must earn their trust by proving that you have their best interests at heart. The easiest way to do this is by "swimming in their tank." This is done by getting out of *your* office area and entering *their* world—go to their turf; have coffee with them; ask them about their concerns, challenges, and frustrations; see where they work; sit in their work area with them; and get to know them. Enter their world. Show interest in their environment.

Once they believe you are interested in them and understand their concerns, they will begin to respond to your concerns. This is not manipulation, it's mutual connection. "Swim in their tank" to get to know them and earn their trust. It will make a big difference in how they respond to you.

Reflection

1. When you meet with a member of your team, do you typically ask him or her to come to your space?

2. When did you last visit your team in their work space when you needed to talk to them?

3. How often do you stop by to visit your team in their work area for short, casual visits with no specific motive?

4. When you are visiting their "tank," do you notice personal mementos, pictures, and awards that tell you what is important to them? These icons reveal their away-from-work life. Show interest in these, and comment on them.

5. Ask a close associate to remind and encourage you to "swim in the tank" of your people regularly.

Gem #20

Doing the same thing the same way will not produce different results.

Related Leadership Dimensions:

Decision Making
Focusing on Results
Problem Solving
Change Management
Innovation

Overview

We are creatures of habit. We often prefer certain ways of doing things. When these methods don't produce the desired results, we become frustrated and disappointed. This is a very normal reaction.

What is interesting about human behavior is that even after not achieving a desired outcome, people tend to do the same thing over and over expecting a different result. It just won't happen. For example, consider the futility of a team leader trying to unite a group of workers by using the exact same methods every week but failing with each repeated attempt. Or, visualize an employee who constantly complains about never being recognized or praised, yet he never changes any aspect of his work such as learning a value added skill, originating an innovative idea, or improving his contribution to the schedule challenges of the organization. Only when new techniques or changed methods are introduced will there be a different result.

One cannot just keep using the exact same approach and achieve a different outcome. The moral is: to expect a different result, some degree of change is required.

Application

Consider a current situation that frustrates you. Perhaps you have a challenging relationship with a peer. Maybe you and your boss do not see eye-to-eye. Or perhaps a key customer informed you that they will not renew a contract. Reflect on what you do—or don't do—that may have contributed to the difficulty in the relationship. Discover what needs to change.

If your primary method of communication is email, try picking up the phone or speaking face-to-face. If you verbalize your criticisms and not your compliments, try reversing it. Identify your usual methods of working with others and if the results aren't what you want, change your methods. The same old behaviors will not improve the situation.

This also applies to handling a challenge in manufacturing, transportation, processing, and financial controls. If you want to improve any aspect of your business or your personal effectiveness, you must try something new. Don't keep doing the same thing and expect different results. It will not happen. Your outcome will never change. You must vary your thinking and your method to achieve your desired result.

Reflection

1. Can you recall situations when you kept getting the same disappointing results time and time again?

2. Reflect on those situations and honestly ask yourself if you altered any of your methods.

3. How does this gem apply to the following: personal and professional relationships, manufacturing processes, sales techniques, department goals, your personal health (weight loss, smoking, exercise), and personal effectiveness as a leader?

4. When trying to increase the overall improvement of a process, system, or relationship, do you overlook the small things? These will make a *major* difference.

5. Ask a trusted colleague to give you objective feedback on small behavioral changes you could make that would give you improved results in various areas.

Gem #21

What you do speaks so loudly that I cannot hear what you say.

Related Leadership Dimensions:

Personal Integrity

Ego Management

Personal Development

Valuing Others

Inspiring Commitment

Overview

We communicate using words. We always have. We always will. Words form the basis of our thoughts. They convey meaning. Words send powerful messages that can inform others and even inspire. But actions always trump words. When leaders' actions are inconsistent with their words, people begin to doubt them. The fact remains that when words and actions contradict, people believe the actions.

When leaders deliver lip service without follow through, cynicism and employee disengagement follow. This is especially detrimental when questionable behavior occurs. It is difficult to win team members' support and loyalty when their leader's behavior does not match what their leader says. The real danger is that trust can be permanently damaged.

When people lose confidence in their leader due to inconsistent, hypocritical behavior, the trust they had in that leader plummets and is very difficult to recover—no matter what the leader says.

Application

Consider the vision or business objectives you advocate to your team or organization. Think about the guiding principles in your own life. We usually pride ourselves in being true to those goals and values, but through the stresses and challenges of life we may fall short of our professed standards of behavior.

When this is done excessively, those around us will place more emphasis on what they observe us doing than what we say. Think of people you know whose words do not mirror their actions. As a result you tend not to trust them. Examine your own behavior. Your inconsistencies will be readily noted. Your associates will see you as hypocritical and will lose respect for you, which severely limits your influence and damages your reputation.

People will note and remember what they observe you doing far more than what you say. The more you "walk the talk," the more others will see you as a leader they want to follow. Your reputation and credibility are at stake.

Reflection

1. Reflect on occasions when you did not follow through with what you said you would do. What were the circumstances? What was the result? What did your people think?

2. Your people will often give you the benefit of the doubt until an observable pattern of negative behavior begins to emerge. If patterns become frequent, they will doubt you. Are your words and actions inconsistent?

3. Consider what you say and do at work. Can you see how your peoples' trust in you is tied to both, but with greater weight on your actions?

4. Ask a confidant who observes your interactions with your team to give you feedback on your level of consistency between what you say and what you do. If there is a serious gap, determine how you can correct it.

5. Write down the personal values you believe in and try to adhere to. Now write down specific ways you will follow these standards in your behavior so you will be consistent, and will therefore be viewed as trustworthy.

Gem #22

Remember the fifth year of the bamboo tree.

Related Leadership Dimensions:

Strategic Thinking

Focusing on Results

Coaching

Personal Development

Team Building

Overview

The bamboo tree has a unique growing cycle. In the first year, one waters and fertilizes the small plant, but nothing happens. The second year, one waters and fertilizes with no noticeable growth. The same pattern continues during the third and fourth years. However, during the fifth year, the bamboo begins to grow rapidly—two feet a day—and in six weeks it reaches ninety feet.

A hasty, superficial glance leads an outsider to believe the efforts of the fifth year led to "magical" growth. However, it is not just the water and fertilizer in the fifth year that helps the bamboo grow. It is the accumulation of five years of careful and consistent attention and nourishment—a combination of water, fertilizer, healthy soil, and ample sunshine—that results in a "sudden" skyward burst.

During the first four years, the bamboo develops a massive underground root structure. If care for the plant is neglected in any single year, then the substantial growth in the fifth year will not occur because the root structure development is impaired. Dedication and consistency with all the essential elements is crucial to achieve its dramatic growth.

Application

Reflect on your level of patience and consistency in developing your people. Yes, it is important to focus on business results that occur today, this week, this month, and this quarter. However, not all business goals mature and demonstrate visible results in such a short period of time.

This is especially true in developing your people. They improve and grow over a longer period and need frequent and consistent coaching, training, encouraging, and nurturing. Consider your focus and frequency in developing your people. They will feel a greater sense of personal worth because you took the time to help them grow.

Set aside time each week to help your team grow their skill sets. This requires time and consistency. Control your impatience. You will not usually see immediate improvement and progress, but over time, with consistent, careful, and focused coaching and attention, your people will grow and develop their potential and capabilities just like the bamboo tree.

Reflection

1. What type of development plan do you have for your people?

2. How high a priority is it—honestly? Do your words match your actions?

3. Are your people included in the design of their development plans?

4. Do you take advantage of times that you are away, such as vacations, business trips, and illness, as an opportunity to give one of your key people responsibility to sit in for you?

5. Like the bamboo, how consistent are you in the efforts, energy, and time you devote to the growth of your people? Discuss with them how they could experience strong growth and improved performance. They must play a primary role in their development plan.

Gem #23

Identify and build your strengths.

Related Leadership Dimensions:

Focusing on Results

Coaching

Ego Management

Personal Development

Overview

*K*now thyself—these profound words, inscribed in the forecourt of the Temple of Apollo at Delphi, have inspired philosophers for centuries. The original author of this phrase is unknown, but the meaning is clear: self-awareness is the first step in maximizing what one can become.

We are fairly good at knowing parts of our capabilities—especially our shortcomings, but we can usually leverage our strengths as well. For instance, as I've coached executives over the years, I have administered work and behavior assessments. When I provide this feedback to them, they tend to focus on their weaknesses or "areas for improvement." They too often ignore their strengths. I remind them that their strengths are 95 percent of the reason they are where they are today.

Sure, we need to be aware of our deficiencies and work to minimize, compensate for, or improve them, but our best efforts should be focused on capitalizing on our strengths—recognizing and developing our full potential. Doing so will lead us to our best performance.

Application

Be aware of your talents and positive capabilities. You will find your greatest satisfaction when your career fully utilizes your strengths. To get to this point, you may want to complete a 360 management feedback instrument, personality assessment, or strengths indicator.

Recall the strengths that your past supervisors or managers have identified in performance reviews. Record moments during the day when you feel especially engaged in your work or successful in what you are doing. Identify what you were doing that helped you feel empowered and accomplished. These sources will help you identify your personal strengths. When you complete a formal assessment, review the results with a focus on the positive attributes.

Build on these strengths and make sure that you have opportunities each day to use them. Do not ignore your blind spots, and seek to minimize their impact. The majority of your focus should be on what you do best. They are your ticket to the future. Take confidence in them, for they are the key to your life's contributions.

Reflection

1. How can you honestly and accurately know what your strengths are? Have you identified your key areas of expertise, your talents, and skills? Knowing these is critical to your confidence and success. Benefit from personal assessments, performance reviews, and objective feedback from coaches and mentors.

2. List three major strengths you have. Are they being used regularly in your current work assignments? How do you capitalize on them? How can you build on them to materialize your plans and dreams?

3. How might your strengths help you overcome or minimize your weaknesses?

4. Ask a trusted colleague to observe how you use your positive capabilities in your job and periodically provide you with useful feedback.

5. Find ways to remind yourself throughout the day of what your strengths are and how you can more completely capitalize on them.

Gem #24

Assign someone to play *the fool*.

Related Leadership Dimensions:

Decision Making

Focusing on Results

Problem Solving

Innovation

Overview

During the European middle ages, the only one in the kingdom who could criticize the king, without losing his head, was the court jester. Another name for him was "the fool."

In the court, the fool played a significant role. He was the clown and everyone laughed at his crazy and bizarre behavior. To the unknowing outsider, he appeared silly, ill behaved, and disrespectful—but in actuality, the fool was often wise, perceptive, and astute. The king knew this, and not only tolerated the fool's brash and outspoken manner, but fully endorsed it because he knew how critical the fool's role was.

The kingdom was filled with sycophants who, with their flattering words, feigned submissiveness to the king. But what of their real thoughts? The fool, through his humorous antics, gave voice to the hidden, unspoken opinions of the people—providing the king with valuable insight. His role was vital to the king and the fool knew it.

Application

As a leader, you have authority and influence that will directly affect other's pay, promotions, job security, and morale. Your people know this. Consequently, there is a natural tendency on their part to please you, to agree with you, and to *appear* to be supportive of your views and opinions.

Opposing ideas are essential for innovation and wise decisions. You need to hear all views. Consider this suggestion: during team meetings, assign someone to play the role of "the fool." It will be his or her job to purposely and obviously take opposing points of view on the subject discussed and potential decisions being considered. Since it is an assigned role, the rest of the team won't begrudge him or her.

The fool is not to be criticized, but rather, encouraged to emphasize contrary and less popular opinions. As a result, everyone will feel more at ease and willing to contribute. Openly voicing all sides during team discussions by purposely employing a little "foolish" behavior will vastly improve your team's decisions.

Reflection

1. When making decisions, how much do you rely on input from others?

2. What techniques do you use to seek out varying opinions from your team?

3. How often do you ask others for their views—especially outsiders who will give you a different perspective?

4. Do you express your views after others have voiced theirs? This avoids the unspoken barrier of "what does the boss think?".

5. Do you assign a random team member to intentionally take an opposing view in a group decision process? This is a vital role that will benefit the entire team. Make sure everyone knows the assigned person is playing "the fool" for the sake of the final outcome. Otherwise, they may think he or she is not a team player.

Gem #25

Allow people the right to fail, but don't sanction incompetence.

Related Leadership Dimensions:

Coaching

Team Building

Valuing Others

Inspiring Commitment

Overview

In the 1930s, an IBM vice-president reporting to Thomas Watson, founder and first president of IBM, had made a $14 million mistake and knew that the boss had called him in to fire him.

As the dreaded meeting convened, the VP was astounded when Watson responded to his offer to resign—since the VP knew he was about to be sacked—by saying: "Fire you? Why should I fire you? I just spent $14 million training you. What's important is to make sure you learn from your mistake and never do it again." Then they discussed and analyzed what had happened so the VP could learn from it.

The executive left Watson's office stunned and grateful. He was also much wiser, more loyal, and had a new determination to be far more careful in his future decisions. Because of Thomas Watson's perspective and foresight, the VP gained an extremely valuable insight into his own strategies, leadership capabilities and potential.

Application

If you never make a mistake, you aren't trying. Allow yourself and others the right to fail. As a leader, make sure you create an environment where mistakes are allowed, but clearly not encouraged. If you don't, the off shoots will include a culture of fear—where creativity and innovation are stifled, and people will hide what they are doing out of fear that they will be caught and punished.

Encourage your people to try new ideas and techniques. Allow them to make mistakes, and then make sure the mistakes are analyzed for maximum learning, so they are not repeated. Let new ideas, methods, processes, and suggestions thrive in your organization.

I have seen organizations where fear was so prevalent that the workers had unspoken procedures in place to cover each other if one made a mistake. Their creative energies were channeled in the wrong direction. Allow your people to make mistakes, but not the same one again and again. Make sure they learn from them. Handled properly, mistakes turn into invaluable learning opportunities.

Reflection

1. What is your patience level when it comes to dealing with mistakes that your people make?

2. Ask yourself if you can honestly see the potential of turning mistakes into insightful and positive experiences that foster learning and growth—both for yourself and others.

3. How do you typically deal with mistakes? Do you sweep them under the carpet or do you confront them directly in an appropriate way so that the learning experience yields greater wisdom and insights?

4. What is the level of fear in your organization? Are your people afraid of what you might do should they make a mistake? If so, they will hide what they do from you, wasting resources, energy and time.

5. How do you reduce the likelihood of the same mistake being repeated? How do you help your people learn from their mistakes?

Gem #26

A leader who stands for everything, stands for nothing.

Related Leadership Dimensions:

Focusing on Results

Personal Integrity

Ego Management

Personal Development

Inspiring Commitment

Overview

Leadership is far from easy. Dealing with multiple, difficult and unpopular issues is daunting. For example, we occasionally observe political leaders who find it difficult to take a firm stand on an issue for fear of alienating a portion of their constituents.

This may also happen when leaders see their support declining, so they shift their stand on issues to broaden their appeal. Business leaders may also do this, especially recently promoted supervisors or executives who want to please all their people. Balancing popular sentiment while maintaining a clear vision is a challenging situation for leaders.

Unfortunately, when leaders focus too much on popular opinion, their direction becomes diluted and unclear. Ironically, overplaying the desire to please decreases the leader's credibility and casts uncertainty in the proper direction to take. This, in turn, may prompt followers to withdraw their support.

Application

Think of the difficult and unpopular issues that you have faced as a leader. Those decisions were probably your most difficult. Think back on how you dealt with that unpleasant dilemma. You were likely tempted to give in to popular opinion even when it might not be the best decision.

Your people watch you as you take on tough decisions. They need to know if they can depend on you to have courage and strength—whether they can truly count on you. Leaders who stand for what they believe in give their people the clear indication of being true to their core values, and can consequently be trusted.

If you find that your level of trust from your people is waning, take an honest look at how you deal with tough issues. Remember, you cannot please everyone. True leaders are able to make uncomfortable decisions that are consistent with their convictions and values. Your people need to know you can be consistently true to what you stand for and then you will earn their trust.

Reflection

1. Can you recall unpopular issues that required you to take an uncomfortable stand? How did you feel? What did you end up doing? What was the result? How did your people respond?

2. Have you ever written down your core values? Do you use them as a standard for your decisions? Identify your convictions.

3. Imagine a plausible situation where you would be pressured into an unwise decision. How do you think you would respond?

4. Consider real or potential issues that you, as a leader, must take a stand on. How might your core values influence the decision you would make regarding these issues?

5. Leadership can be lonely. To what extent do you worry about pleasing the people around you? Is your desire to please others negatively impacting your decisions and actions?

Gem #27

Greatness is not where you stand, but the direction you are moving.

Related Leadership Dimensions:

Customer Focus

Focusing on Results

Coaching

Personal Development

Team Building

Change Management

Overview

Successful professionals often have enviable track records. Unfortunately, they may be tempted to live in the past, relying on their reputations and previous accomplishments. They may also live only in the present, satisfied with the status quo.

This can discourage personal growth, prevent additional development of their leadership skills, and block learning innovative ways of addressing and solving ever-evolving future challenges. Some leaders had achieved greatness "back then," but what have they done lately? As a result, they can become obstacles or blockers to the organization, earning the military label of "ROAD" meaning "Retired-On-Active-Duty." Living in the past, they lose their competitive edge, which is essential for future success.

Just as limiting is living only in the present with little thought toward preparing for the future. This is just as unproductive as focusing on the past.

The past and present are important in reinforcing skills and confidence, but the future demands staying current through non-stop improvement. One's direction determines the critical course of action. Forward motion provides vital preparation for future greatness.

Application

What we perceive as "greatness" is often fleeting. To truly earn that remarkable label requires continuous effort and diligence. In studying those who are widely regarded as "great" in any field, we discover that they worked at personal improvement consistently for many years—and never stopped working.

Take an honest look in the mirror. Consider where you are you headed. Review your goals. Determine the extent to which you are relying on your past or present. It is essential to reach personal milestones throughout your life, and not just at an earlier stage. Keep looking forward, gathering the skills and knowledge along the way that will prepare you for the uncertainties of the future.

Sustained effort, personal awareness, and focused progress—especially in helping others succeed—will bring you lasting and meaningful recognition and greatness.

Reflection

1. Do you regularly evaluate where you are and what you will need in the future?

2. Do you regularly participate in assessment programs that provide feedback to allow you to see yourself as others see you?

3. How well do you know your strengths? How well are you capitalizing on them?

4. How would you benefit from engaging an objective coach or mentor to honestly counsel you and help you polish your skills?

5. How well do you learn from mistakes and errors of judgment? How can you learn from these and apply them to future decisions? Shift your focus from the past to the future.

Gem #28

Prescription without diagnosis is malpractice.

Related Leadership Dimensions:

Strategic Thinking
Decision Making
Problem Solving
Change Management

Overview

Even if we didn't go to medical school or work in a pharmacy, we all know that a doctor needs to carefully examine a patient and study the symptoms before prescribing medications.

The initial exam may lead to additional tests, lab work, or X-rays to pinpoint the cause of the pain or other symptoms. For the doctor to rely solely on instinct or assumption, without proper examination, will most likely lead to a flawed diagnosis, which in turn leads to an incorrect prescription, and possibly malpractice and severe harm to the patient.

Imagine going to a doctor with a problem, only to have the physician just hand you a bottle of pills without even exploring your symptoms. You would naturally be frustrated and doubtful it would help.

The process of discovering a correct treatment plan cannot be found without first accurately identifying the problem which requires time and study. To do otherwise is foolish and even dangerous.

Application

We are living in a world that requires rushed decisions. Everyone wants everything to happen now. This seems to be the case in every aspect of our busy and frantic lives. In all the haste, there is sometimes little room for careful and vital analysis. Yet, speedy and rushed decisions are unwise and can likely produce disappointing results.

When you sense there is pressure on you to come up with a hasty outcome, *slow* down. You must conduct the requisite investigation, gather the facts, and examine the situation *before* a decision is made. You owe that to your superiors, your team, your customers, your career, and your own integrity.

Whenever possible, take the time to perform an analysis of relevant facts. Then you will be in a far better position to determine the best course of action or prescription. This is a sure-fire recipe to avoid malpractice, harm, and injury.

Reflection

1. Do you have a tendency to instinctively make emotional or knee-jerk decisions in response to sudden situations or problems?

2. How quickly do you feel your work situation requires you to make important decisions?

3. What percentage of your decision-making time is spent gathering relevant data *before* action is taken?

4. How can you change your natural inclination of hurrying decisions so that you will slow down and be more careful, and perform the necessary study?

5. Identify the types of information you typically need in order to make a prudent and informed decision, such as data needed, money, time, consequences, and people involved?

Gem #29

Every transaction
begins with
a relationship.

Related Leadership Dimensions:

Customer Focus
Ego Management
Listening
Team Building
Valuing Others
Organizational Savvy

Overview

Every transaction begins with a relationship between parties. Each has a need, idea or agenda and each shares it with the other. When it appears to benefit both parties, the first steps to a contract or purchase occur.

As the mutual satisfaction of the arrangement increases, so does the strength of the relationship. Consequently, as the strength of the relationship grows so will the likelihood of a repeated transaction.

The opposite is also true. When one party does anything to diminish the trust of the other or acts in his or her own self-interest without regard for the other, the relationship is damaged and future transactions are threatened and are at risk.

The goal should be to build and strengthen relationships to increase the likelihood of future transactions. Our reputation, credibility, and business depend on it.

Application

We agree that the reputation we enjoy with our business associates is critical. This is the foundation of all future transactions. Consider past customer relationships that endured and those that did not. You will likely observe that mutual satisfaction was an essential ingredient for the successful ones.

This was influenced by trust, characterized by meeting expectations of quality, schedule, and cost. However, it was also influenced by your ability to listen to their needs and to be responsive and flexible. Consider what you can do to build stronger relationships with your customers. For example, dialogue openly and honestly with your key customers. Ask them how you can better meet their needs. Genuinely demonstrate your interest in their concerns and priorities.

Your ability to preserve, nourish and strengthen the relationship you have with them will directly determine the likelihood of future transactions. This should be your primary focus. Remember, it all starts with a relationship.

Reflection

1. How often do you carefully analyze each of your primary customer relationships?

2. Do you have any reliable feedback from your customers about their perception of your overall service?

3. When you learn about a negative aspect of your customer relationships, how do you address it?

4. How often do you put yourself in the shoes of your customers and imagine what they experience with you?

5. What do you currently do to proactively maintain good relationships with your customers? Are there other things you could and should do to better meet their concerns, priorities and needs?

Gem #30

Activity
vs.
Results

Related Leadership Dimensions:

Dependability

Focusing on Results

Personal Development

Time Management

Overview

The British philosopher, William George Jordan, describes the term "hurry" as a counterfeit that "seeks ever to make energy a substitute for a clearly defined plan."

It's easy to be busy. We too often become distracted by many things that seem interesting or appear to be urgent, but may actually distract us from our—or our boss's—long-term goals. We get caught in the trap of convincing ourselves that we are productive because we are crossing many items off of our lists. However, too often we are actually adding easy or unimportant tasks just so we can draw a line through them. This leads to critical activities or tasks being continually transferred to the next day's to-do list.

The habit of filling open time slots with needless minutia and idle discussions can sap energy and time. We may fool ourselves into thinking we are productive, but at the end of the day, are we really accomplishing what is truly important? We may believe we are delivering "results" when we are just engaging in "activity."

Application

Consider conducting an honest self-assessment of how you use your time and energy. Decide how you can spend more of your scarce resource of time focusing on the tasks that matter most. To do this, define the essentials, the truly significant ones—the things that *must* be done. Think of what is absolutely important to you, your boss, your business, your customers (internal and external), and those who are significant in your personal life.

Try an experiment for a few days by logging how you spend each hour of your day. Then identify what you actually accomplish. Tracking your day will increase your awareness of activities that rob your time. It will help you identify less important activities that prevent you from achieving what you truly desire. Then identify what actions you want to stop, start, or continue doing.

This will help you gain control of your "busy-ness" by being more strategic about how you spend your time. Being more purposeful with your time will enhance your ability to deliver your desired results—"essential" will replace "busy!"

Reflection

1. Do you find that your boss and your team express disappointment with your output, even though you seem to be always "busy"? If so, this gem is particularly applicable to you and your work methods.

2. Follow the suggestion of keeping a time log for a few days to identify how you use your time. What "busy" tasks are getting in the way of "essential" tasks? How can you be more strategic in your use of time?

3. Identify others who use their time well. Have a candid discussion with them about how they do it. Identify the techniques you can adopt from them.

4. Ask your supervisor how you could become more responsive to the tasks assigned to you. At the very least, your boss will likely be impressed with your eagerness to improve.

5. Write down the goals of your work group. These are clearly defined objectives that will help you focus your time and resources in doing your part to achieve them.

Gem #31

The most important game of the season is the next one.

Related Leadership Dimensions:

Customer Focus

Focusing on Results

Coaching

Team Building

Inspiring Commitment

Overview

Every sports team dreams of winning the championship game. The key element in doing so is to recognize that every *little* game is a critical part of getting to the *big game*. The same is true in business.

An essential part of leading is setting a clear direction for the group. This involves balancing short-term plans with long-term strategy. It involves setting priorities, establishing and reaching milestones, meeting deadlines, and staying within budget. While any team wants to be successful, focusing only on the championship game or final completion of the project is not a wise or successful approach. Instead, the most important short-term step is preparing for and achieving each "next" milestone.

This will keep the *focus* where it should be, and will minimize slip-ups. Making sure that each intermediate step is effectively and successfully accomplished is the only way to achieve the long-term objective. Yes, preparing for match-ups with your traditional rivals or other big games is important, but your current focus should always be on the next one. A team that looks past the next game, may never reach the big one. The underestimated "no sweat" small game may in fact beat you—crushing your hopes for the championship.

Application

Consider how you prioritize what your team works on. Your first action should be to identify the most critical steps to accomplishing your long-term goals. Ensure that you and your team are focused on the activities that matter most—the *next* sale or reaching the *next* step in a research and development program. Every intermediate milestone is critical.

Establish clear and complete project plans and sales targets with deadlines and owners. Establish regular status updates to provide feedback and spotlight the most important activities for each week. A good leader effectively prioritizes what is most important, monitors energy and resources spent on projects, and guides the team toward hitting every milestone toward the "big" target.

Align performance with the long-term vision, and then put all of your effort on *today's* operations—in that order. Then your team is more likely to play in the championship game because they will have "won" every game leading to it.

Reflection

1. Have you and your team clearly identified your overall objective?

2. Have you and your team defined the intermediate steps and milestones toward the overall objective?

3. Once the above two essential steps are determined, how do you ensure that you and your team remain focused on each intermediate step? What are typical interruptions that can derail your focus? What do you underestimate?

4. Do you recognize how essential each intermediate step is, and that skipping or missing any of these seriously impacts the entire principal objective?

5. How do you help the team to maintain their focus and efforts on the next "game"—the next phase or step of the task—rather than worrying about the final outcome? What additional methods would help you and your team maintain focus on the intermediate steps?

Gem #32

A fish rots
from the
head down.

Related Leadership Dimensions:

Dependability
Personal Integrity
Coaching
Inspiring Commitment
Organizational Savvy

Overview

Early cultures who relied on fish as their primary diet ate the head first because only the body could be stored for long periods of time. They knew the head rotted first. This has great appication to the impact of a leader.

The leader is the single most powerful influence on an organization. The leader's actions send strong messages to others—especially to direct reports—about what is important to the team and to the company.

Many successes and failures can be traced back to the decisions, reactions, behavior, and attitudes of the leader. Sometimes it is easy to look at the team as the problem, but the more accurate focus is to first look at the leader. Just as a fish rots from the head down, a poor team is often the result of weak leadership.

What message do leaders send to their teams by their demeanor, frame of mind, and capability? What examples are they setting? Do they truly practice what they preach? It all starts with the head of the fish—the leader!

Application

Examine the effectiveness of your team. Consider how your team achieves the desired results. Analyze how often the appropriate information gets passed to the right people. Make sure your team norms support the direction of the company. Before accusing or finding fault with your people, ask yourself what *you* can do differently.

I have seen countless teams or departments that were struggling in a variety of ways. Close scrutiny revealed that the leader was nearly always the primary cause.

Look at the attitude you project. Identify your true motivation and personal drive. Consider how you involve others in decision making. Remain consistent to a clearly stated purpose and remember to champion and develop your people.

Ask your team for their feedback. Discuss the behaviors you want to improve. Seek their input. Describe the actions you will take and ask for their support. These practices will help you be a more effective leader, and will create a stronger team.

Reflection

1. Who do you blame when your team's performance does not meet your expectations?

2. It is very easy to look at substandard performance by individuals on your team, but you must also take an honest look at *yourself* to see how you could do better.

3. Do you approach your responsibilities from the belief that it is acceptable for leaders to *not* have all the answers, and to rely on input from team members to resolve issues? If not, how can you improve?

4. Do you take full and sincere advantage of personal development opportunities to refine your leadership skills?

5. Ask a trusted mentor, coach, or supervisor for counsel and assistance in helping you grow in your overall leadership capabilities.

Gem #33

Just when you think you are winning the rat race, along comes a faster rat!

Related Leadership Dimensions:

Coaching
Personal Development
Change Management
Innovation

Overview

Andy Grove, founder and former president of Intel, wrote a book on the history of his tenure at the successful computer chip maker. It is entitled, *Only the Paranoid Survive*.

The book's title sends a strong message on how to manage in today's marketplace. One must never become complacent and stagnant. Success can be fleeting. Constant focus on competitors and market forces is essential to maintaining success. However, while few may dispute this statement, it is easy and common to be lulled into feeling overconfident. This is true for organizations, teams, and individuals.

Leaders need to keep in mind that a faster, better, cheaper product or service is often just around the corner. This is also true of people—positions are never guaranteed. Both people and organizations need to be prepared for that reality and not become too confident or comfortable with their current situation.

Application

Personally, look at the degree of stagnation that may be creeping into your own development. To what extent are you becoming complacent? How do you stay current? Take full advantage of opportunities to polish and refine your skills, talents, and strengths to help you stay competitive. Be aware of your blind spots that are impeding your effectiveness both interpersonally and organizationally.

As the team leader, who do you recognize for great performance? Think about how you reward adaptability, innovation, and forward-thinking. These are critical skills that will keep you and your team nimble, responsive, and ahead of the pack. Do all you can to eliminate complacency among your people. Change the atmosphere with a strong results-oriented culture.

By focusing on yourself and your team to remain competitive, you will stay ahead of the "rats" that are trying to take your place.

Reflection

1. In your organization, how much do you emphasize innovation and how do you sustain that attitude?

2. Who are your closest competitors? What are they doing to try to overtake your customers and market share? How are you countering their efforts?

3. What specifically are you doing to stay competitive and at the top of your game? How often do you update and modify your tool kit?

4. Seriously and frequently review and analyze industry trends. Pay close attention to those that compete against you. How are you staying ahead of them? Be alert for small signs leading to major change.

5. Do you find yourself (personally and professionally) being more proactive or reactive to life? If you are reactive, you may find that your job or your organization may become obsolete. Being proactive will keep you ahead of the race.

Gem #34

Plan and achieve small wins.

Related Leadership Dimensions:

Focusing on Results

Team Building

Change Management

Inspiring Commitment

Organizational Savvy

Overview

Change is a constant in our lives. This is especially true in organizations. Employees have to respond to reorganizations, increased job responsibilities, new methods and processes, more efficient procedures, cost savings, new assignments . . . the list goes on.

The sum total of these can have a huge downward impact on morale. A good leader is aware of this, and strategically weaves into the mix ways to enable the team to experience *genuine* small wins. These victories, properly recognized with small celebrations, are vital to raising morale and helping the team realize that progress is being made.

Without these wins, a subtle feeling of being overwhelmed can creep over the group and lead to doubts and discouragement. Providing small wins will build morale, promote enthusiasm, and sustain commitment. Motivation will thrive as your team moves along the long road toward the ultimate objective. People need to see and believe that they are making progress. They need encouragement. A good leader will champion their efforts.

Application

Take a look at your team and your organization. Notice major and minor changes such as—new approaches, different procedures, and job adjustments that they have been asked to make over the past several months. See if job descriptions have increased in scope. Determine if delivery schedules have been tightened or if job security pressures have increased.

All of this can increase stress and decrease morale for employees. You, as the leader, should purposefully design small but genuine wins that the team can achieve to keep morale high. Go for the low-hanging fruit—the reachable victories such as quick milestones reached, schedules outlined, budgets designed, or key positions filled. Be creative. Once they hit small targets, *celebrate*!

A string of these small victories will do wonders toward building team spirit, growing morale, and generating internal hunger to achieve more and stay the course, as difficult as it is. The pressure of responding to endless changes will seem much more plausible to the workforce. Energy and commitment will return. They will see their progress. They will feel and act like winners—because they see that they are winners!

Reflection

1. Are you able to clearly define the BIG overarching objective that your team has been asked to accomplish? Once that is clear, are you able to break that down into achievable smaller steps?

2. With these smaller steps, what small wins can you envision for your team to achieve?

3. How can you direct these small wins so they actually occur? (Remember that they must be *genuine*, or they will see through it—as phony or contrived.)

4. When these small wins occur, how do you celebrate them? Celebrations should not require much budget, and often require none.

5. As your team achieves small wins, monitor their attitudes and morale so you can see how important these minor victories are. Keep close track of the team's "pulse."

Gem #35

They won't remember what you said, but they will remember how you made them feel.

Related Leadership Dimensions:

Effective Communication

Presentation Skills

Team Building

Valuing Others

Inspiring Commitment

Overview

Leaders and managers at all levels give speeches, have meetings, and participate in formal and informal gatherings. The message they deliver may not always be remembered, but the way it is delivered will have a major impact on how everyone feels.

With all of the messages people receive and all the activities people do, it is a challenge to remember everything. Even though people have difficulty recalling what they heard in a meeting or read in an email, they usually remember how they felt when a leader spoke or wrote to them.

They remember the tone, mood, intensity, degree of sincerity, and attitude of the interaction far more than the subject covered. One's emotional response is a powerful reaction that rarely goes unnoticed and can linger far longer than the content of a spoken or written message. Thus, *what* leaders say is important, but *how* they say it can leave a strong and lasting impression.

Application

When you make a presentation or participate in a group discussion, pay careful attention to *how* you convey your thoughts.

Consider how you communicate key messages. Your nonverbal gestures, tone, facial expression, and sincerity all convey strong impressions. More importantly, these elements work together to influence how people respond to you.

Consider your attitude at the time of the communication. Imagine a leader who looks away when others speak during interactions or has a serious and overly intense manner when speaking. Negative non-verbal gestures and moods may leave people feeling unappreciated.

Consider the feelings of others as you craft your communication. Convey the right emotions and not just the right words. Your people will remember how they felt, far longer than they remember what you said.

Reflection

1. Think of feedback you have received from groups you have presented to. What was their reaction? What did you learn?

2. Are you aware of how you made them feel?

3. Pay attention to your nonverbal cues such as eyes, gestures, body language, tone, and sincerity.

4. As you present or interact with others, are you aware of their concerns, needs, and feelings? How can you adapt your attitude and style in response to their feelings?

5. The next time you present to a group, try to record it so you can watch and see what your audience saw. This is an excellent opportunity for unfiltered feedback.

Gem #36

Obstacles are
things you see
when you take
your eye off
the goal.

Related Leadership Dimensions:

Strategic Thinking

Problem Solving

Focusing on Results

Change Management

Inspiring Commitment

Overview

As we move through life, we have special dreams we hope to turn into reality. These dreams, analyzed carefully, become a series of goals which establish a clear and desired endpoint. Identifying a target can be motivating because it defines the finish line and clearly states what success along the way toward that goal will look like.

Problems or issues inevitably arise in pursuing the goal. These obstacles must not be ignored. It would be foolish to not acknowledge and address them. However, too much attention on them becomes distracting, frustrating, and demoralizing. When your eyes and efforts remain focused on the initial objective, these stumbling blocks lose their intimidation, and actually allow you to make adjustments and recalibrate.

When viewed in a different light, hurdles become stepping stones. These barriers and challenges can then be greeted with purpose and energy instead of discouragement and fatigue. The obstacles, in effect, become opportunities that provide assistance and support along the path to completing your goal which allows you to make a dream come true.

Application

Write down your dreams. Break them up into specific steps or goals on paper that you can focus on. Start a habit of capturing these goals and regularly referencing them. Share them with a mentor, confidant, or trusted friend to receive their encouragement.

As obstacles arise, use your support network to check your reaction to your goals. These obstacles can be viewed as either barriers or opportunities. Think of them as checkpoints on the path to your goal. Do this when problems are small; it can prevent unnecessary frustration and angst.

Consider the times you get discouraged or distracted. There might be a recurring theme or situation that causes you to take your eyes off of your target. Identify ways of minimizing or avoiding these pitfalls, so you can keep your focus on your goal and your efforts on accomplishment. Then you will hit your target.

Reflection

1. How consistently and regularly do you set and review your personal and professional goals?

2. Do you share them with a confidant or mentor? They can provide needed support.

3. As you try to achieve your goal, how do you view the speed bumps or roadblocks that impede your progress?

4. What are the times, reasons, or people that seem to bring on obstacles? Do you see a pattern?

5. Identify methods that will help you go around, avoid or put in proper perspective these obstacles so you can meet your goals.

Gem #37

A desk is a
dangerous place
from which to
view the world.

Related Leadership Dimensions:

Coaching

Listening

Valuing Others

Inspiring Commitment

Organizational Savvy

Overview

The transition from individual contributor to leader is a difficult one. Your employees and team members are typically focused on their own results, their own schedule, and their own needs.

Because their jobs do not require them to be as concerned with the big picture, they often don't get out of their cube or office to see what is *really* happening. They usually aren't monitoring attitudes, learning of issues, or providing feedback to others—like the leader must do.

Becoming a leader involves *being* with others. Leaders must circulate among their people to understand their concerns and challenges, remove roadblocks, encourage, clarify, support and teach. Remaining at one's desk may have brought safety and success as an individual contributor, but as a leader you need a more broad and scenic view. Leaders must be out among their people.

Application

Consider how much time you spend at your desk or in your office. How often do you get out and walk and talk with your people?

I once observed a director who rarely left his office. He relied on email and instant messages to communicate with his people, even though they were close by. His people felt distant and unsupported and were reluctant to voice concerns. He gradually grew out of touch with what was really happening. He was failing as a leader.

Make an effort regularly to stop by and see your employees. When doing so, avoid being their "monitor," just observe their world and ask them how you can better support them. You will learn of events, attitudes, issues, challenges, and concerns that you would have been insulated from by staying in your office. The information and awareness you gain will prove invaluable!

As a result, you will be far more in touch, and more effective and responsive to what is happening to your organization. You will have a more accurate outlook and perspective of your people and your stewardship. You will be a stronger leader.

Reflection

1. How often in an average day or week do you leave your regular routine and mingle among your people?

2. Do you rely solely on your own perspective and exposure when you are making a key decision?

3. Are you aware of the concerns of others? How do you know? There is much-needed information out there that your direct reports may *not* be sharing in your staff meeting. Go find it.

4. How often do you engage in meaningful conversation with others in your organization who you do not regularly see?

5. Determine ways to leave your own office area more frequently to allow you to talk to others. Doing so will send the message that you care, are available, and are in touch with them.

Gem #38

Just because you are good with a hammer gives you no right to view the world as a bunch of nails.

Related Leadership Dimensions:

Coaching
Personal Development
Team Building
Valuing Others
Inspiring Commitment

Overview

Skilled construction workers use a variety of tools during the building process. Consider how ridiculous and useless it would be if they used only a hammer for each task.

As leaders acquire habits and gain knowledge, they develop a versatile bag of tools and approaches. These tools provide great value and can dramatically increase a leader's success. However, when leaders become so good at applying a certain style, they are more inclined to use that style even when it is not the right one for a particular situation.

Leaders sometimes force a situation to fit the method or tool they prefer instead of being flexible and allowing the circumstances to determine the right skill or tool to be used.

Application

Consider the various tools in your leadership tool box. Do you favor certain approaches or philosophies? Is there a chance that the one you usually use is not always the best fit? If you are used to starting or building a business, the tools you once used may no longer be the most effective when you are required to grow a successful business.

When dealing with people, perhaps you prefer an authoritative leadership style. This style may often work, but can be ineffective when the situation demands a high level of buy-in and employee engagement. In leadership, limited approaches yield limited results. You need to be proficient with a number of styles.

Open yourself to feedback from others as you consider your usual responses to various circumstances. Because of the large variety of personalities and situations you face, you must learn to monitor the use of your typical methods. Be flexible and adaptable. This will help you put down your hammer when no nails exist and apply a more appropriate style or skill. Flexibility will be your mantra.

Reflection

1. Are you aware of your primary or dominant leadership style?

2. When might you need to use a secondary or alternative style? What reminders do you need to remember that your natural style isn't always the most appropriate?

3. Do you recognize that each member of your team has different backgrounds, personalities, and needs?

4. Can you see that using the same approach on all of your people is not going to achieve the desired results because of their varied makeup?

5. Recall feedback you have received over time regarding your leadership style and the impact it has on others. Have you tried to implement that feedback? How did it improve your interactions with others? Analyze those results to allow you to have greater flexibility in working with others.

Gem #39

Change is bad until it succeeds.

Related Leadership Dimensions:

Customer Focus

Focusing on Results

Change Management

Innovation

Inspiring Commitment

Organizational Savvy

Overview

People often resist change, especially when it is first proposed. It does not seem to matter how much sense the new change makes. It may save money, increase efficiency, improve quality, ensure quicker turn-around time, or serve the customer better. Despite these benefits, there is an innate resistance to the change by those who will be affected by it.

This reaction is typical of human nature. We are creatures of habit and routine. Anything that takes us out of our comfort zone is "bad" or "scary," and we usually reject it with a litany of reasons why "it won't work."

Think of the widely accepted innovations that are now part of mainstream life today that, when originally proposed, were thought to be ridiculous or even crazy. Yet, given time, people got used to them, and eventually could not live without them. They ended up embracing change.

Application

As leaders, you will find yourself on both sides of change—either a new policy that will directly affect you or a new procedure that you are to promote and implement with others. These may include a change to the organization's structure, compensation, processes, systems, administrative policies, employee benefits, cost savings, or a myriad of other "new" changes.

As you face these, recall the changes of the past that you were a part of. Remember how the initial reaction to them was often negative. However, once it was implemented and it actually proved successful, people saw the value of it and even supported it. Be patient as others initially resist the change you are promoting.

Consider three successful techniques when implementing change: 1) listen to their concerns, 2) explain the business case for the change, and 3) build small wins to gradually demonstrate the rationale behind the change. These three simple steps will likely affect even the most ardent opponent to begin the transition from "this is awful" to "this actually might work, make my life better, and I can live with it!"

Reflection

1. How do you initially respond to change at work?

2. How do others you work with (boss, peers, direct reports, and other associates) typically respond to change?

3. How patient do you tend to be you with others as they experience change? Can you relate to their objections?

4. How do you follow up to ensure others understand the reasons behind the change? Are you sensitive to the need for clear and open communication to promote understanding? The more extensive the change, the greater the need for increased communication.

5. Try to build small wins to show the benefits of change.

Gem #40

How you *respond* is the real test.

Related Leadership Dimensions:

Personal Integrity

Problem Solving

Coaching

Ego Management

Personal Development

Inspiring Commitment

Overview

Life is full of uncertainties. We never know what challenges we will face next. Yet one of life's certainties is that we all make mistakes. This applies equally to ourselves as well as others. The critical question then is *how will you respond to mistakes?*

We do our best to make good decisions, follow wise plans, engage in smart investments, use sound judgment, and learn from past mistakes. However, our lives are filled with minor and major regrets as a result of poor choices, hasty decisions, stressful behaviors, and external factors.

Often we must face up to disappointing results that we are responsible for. But there are also unpleasant and disappointing situations that are not our fault. We cannot always control or prevent these unfortunate occurrences. The challenge in both cases becomes our reaction to them—*how we respond.*

Application

As you consider your own professional and even personal life, think of the ways you respond to disappointments.

Examine how you deal with sub par performance from yourself or from your associates. It is natural for blood pressure to rise, stress to increase, and emotion to take over. In times of stress we revert back to our natural tendencies. Unfortunately, it is the unbridled release of these "natural tendencies" that can cause us to have serious regret once the emotional dust has settled.

This gem also applies to how we respond to positive events such as winning a contract, getting promoted, and beating out a competitor. Our attitude and behavior will speak volumes to others about our character.

When you face major challenges—either by your own doing or someone else's—just remember that how we respond to what happens is far more important than what actually happens. At the end of the day, *that choice* will make all the difference between regret and satisfaction. You have the individual power to select the outcome by what you do when mistakes and disappointments happen. Your response will speak loudly to others, and will define your character.

Reflection

1. What is your typical response when you make a mistake?

2. Do you have a tendency to blame others?

3. How much ownership do you take for your own actions? Others will notice this.

4. Consider asking a trusted associate to provide you with honest feedback regarding how you respond to errors or mistakes of varying magnitudes.

5. Do you recognize that making mistakes can end up being a remarkable learning opportunity that may positively impact future situations? It all depends on how you respond to them.

Gem #41

You can buy
hands and feet,
but you must earn
the heart.

Related Leadership Dimensions:

Coaching

Listening

Personal Development

Team Building

Valuing Others

Inspiring Commitment

Overview

Leaders can hire someone for minimum wage or $20 an hour or even $200 an hour. But all they are likely to get are the employee's hands and feet.

Your people may be physically present, but too often all they give is the bare minimum, resulting in little commitment to the job. This type of employee becomes a "clock-watcher," eagerly waiting for quitting time each day, living for the weekend, and dreading Sunday night because the next day is a "lousy work day." They have emotionally checked out. Clearly something is missing—their heart.

Hands and feet can be bought, the heart must be earned. The heart determines commitment, which leads to performance. The heart is earned through consistent time and effort by the leader. Only when hearts are combined with hands will an organization maximize its success.

Application

Consider the commitment level of your own employees and team members. Determine whether they are giving more than just the bare minimum.

Think of their attitude toward achieving the team's goals and objectives. Evaluate their capacity and the extent to which they are contributing their full potential to your organization. You may have only their hands and feet. It is likely that you have not earned their hearts.

Earning the heart is achieved by leader-driven behaviors that go far beyond a paycheck. These include providing additional job challenges, asking for opinions and *listening* to them, helping team members feel valued, stretching their capacity, and recognizing their growth and contributions in front of their peers. When leaders genuinely care about their people, then their people's hearts will follow.

Earning the heart will strengthen your team and lead to increased performance—from individuals and from the team as a whole.

Reflection

1. Do you believe you have earned your people's hearts? Why or why not?

2. Do you believe that your people could contribute to your goals or objectives more than they currently do?

3. In what ways could the environment you have established be contributing to their lack of commitment to performance?

4. How could you help your people feel more valued?

5. What behaviors, mannerisms, or practices could you refine or improve to enhance your ability to earn their hearts?

Gem #42

Give them the ball and let them run with it.

Related Leadership Dimensions:

Delegating

Focusing on Results

Ego Management

Team Building

Inspiring Commitment

Overview

Many sports involve one player giving the ball to another. How ridiculous would it be if the player making the handoff kept hold of the ball as the intended teammate tried to take it. If this happened, the confused recipient would be yelling, "Hey, let go! Let me take it! I can't run with it as long as you are hanging on to the ball!"

In the world of athletics, this situation rarely occurs on successful teams. However, in the world of organizations, the above scenario is not uncommon. For example, a manager assigns a task to a direct report, but keeps hovering over him because of lingering doubts about the employee's competence. As a result, the employee senses his supervisor's doubts, is annoyed by the micromanaging style and is frustrated. Both the delegator and the receiver look foolish, and the task may not get done properly.

Delegated tasks are too often muddied with mistrust, doubts, and uncertainty. The frequent result is a fumble. Unfortunately, this negatively impacts the desired performance now and in the future. Everyone loses.

Application

Honestly evaluate your tendency to hold on to tasks that you have delegated to others. If you feel that you don't have confidence in them, you will hang on to the assignment yourself and nullify any good that could have been accomplished by delegating it.

In such a case, your colleague will not be able to run with it, will likely feel frustrated, and will sense your lack of trust. When delegated tasks or assignments do not go as you expect, you must evaluate whether or not you really let your colleague have ownership of the task.

Less experienced employees need more supervision, but your senior people expect you to give them the task completely and then get out of the way. Be available for them, but let them run with the ball without the added baggage of your doubts and hesitation. At the end of the day, they will surprise you with what they are able to accomplish, and you will be free to do those actions only you can do.

Reflection

1. Do you believe that your willingness to properly delegate comes down to a trust issue? What can you do to increase your willingness to trust others?

2. If there are members of your team that you do not fully trust to run with the tasks you must delegate to them, what are the reasons for your lack of trust? What can you do to turn this around?

3. Once you have identified the reasons, determine methods that could help your people improve in the areas in which they are deficient.

4. Are you willing to have an open and honest discussion with your team members regarding how future delegated tasks could be completed more smoothly and effectively?

5. Put yourself in the shoes of your employees and ask yourself: "What is it like to be on the receiving end of a delegated assignment from me?" This may really open your eyes to their point-of-view.

Gem #43

Silence is
your ally,
not
your enemy.

Related Leadership Dimensions:

Effective Communication
Decision Making
Problem Solving
Ego Management
Listening
Personal Development

Overview

Too often during conversations, leaders feel uncomfortable with silence. A few seconds of quiet and leaders may instinctively fill that awkward silence with talk.

It is helpful to remember that silence is a normal part of communication, not an anomaly. Silence can be a powerful method of allowing others to pause and think, fully express their ideas, divulge real concerns, convey insightful feedback, and add meaningful information to an elusive solution.

Smart leaders add "silence" to their communication tool kit, which enables them to learn from their associates. Silence provides time for information to be processed and allows moments of reflection before giving a response. Using silence appropriately sends the message that you value a person's opinion enough to wait for it, listen to it, and consider it. Combining your people's thoughts to your views can make a powerful combination.

Application

Consider how you respond to silence during one-on-one conversations with your people or in a team meeting. When you are impatient or frustrated by silence, you may feel compelled to fill the silence by talking.

Silence is a friend. Get to know it. Practice using it. Become confident with it. Recognize that it is a reliable tool. After you ask a question or make a statement, pause for 5 seconds. This may seem like an eternity, but it opens up mental space for others to think and then respond to you with what is on their mind.

As a result, you will have increased access to your people's views, opinions, and ideas—PLUS, they will feel valued because you welcome their input.

Silence is powerful. Effectively using this conversational tool will improve your ability to lead others to higher levels of quality performance. An effective leader knows when to speak, when to listen, and when to employ silence.

Reflection

1. Are you aware of the amount of silence that you tend to use in your general conversations?

2. Are you comfortable with moments of silence or do you feel you must fill them with verbiage?

3. Consider when and why silence makes you uncomfortable. Then decide how you can overcome those barriers in order to improve your ability to use silence in your conversations.

4. Think of others you may have observed who use silence effectively—how and when do they use it? Watch them and learn to incorporate their behaviors.

5. Identify techniques and reminders to help you use appropriate silence more often. Ask a trusted colleague or mentor to watch you in meetings or conversations and provide feedback and suggestions.

Gem #44

A turtle moves
only after it
first sticks its
neck out.

Related Leadership Dimensions:

Focusing on Results
Coaching
Personal Development
Change Management
Innovation
Inspiring Commitment

Overview

Turtles' hard shells are a great source of protection. But they can't move if they stay inside of these protective shells. Their legs and heads must extend beyond the confines of the shell. This is risky, but necessary. Movement and progress involves risk. "Shells" represent a safety zone, and employees may feel uncomfortable stepping outside of it.

It is usually safer to stay within one's shell, so leaders must create an environment where people will shed their shells and become involved—free from fear. This is vital when industries, companies, and teams need to act and change quickly. A leader needs to assert new ideas and follow up with behaviors that let people know they will not be harmed if they "come out of their shells."

Without willingness to stick one's neck out, positive action and results will not happen. Leaders must foster an environment that rewards innovation and welcomes appropriate risks. Their people must feel comfortable and confident to come out of their shells and fully contribute.

Application

Evaluate your personal comfort level with risk. Consider how you respond to ideas that are outside the mainstream and your willingness to share innovative thoughts. Are you ridiculed for expressing these ideas or are you encouraged and supported?

Your people are likely to have similar feelings. Think of things you can do that would help your organization or team to leave their protective "shells." Be willing to talk with them about innovative ways of solving problems or addressing challenges. Identify the topics they may dodge and reasons for this avoidance. Observe their level of confidence and willingness to move out of the safety of their shells.

In my experience, many professionals who offered successful and well-received ideas were initially reluctant to do so out of fear that they would appear foolish. But when they were encouraged and not put down, they responded favorably.

Learn from your own experience—help your people to ignore the tendency to remain secure in their shells. Develop their ability to be more willing to stick their necks out. This is when your organization will *really* move forward.

Reflection

1. What is your personal tolerance for risk? (Total avoidance? Low? Moderate? High?)

2. Are you comfortable enough with risk or change to suggest it in front of others? Your people likely have similar feelings.

3. Your associates are likely to feel hesitant to express new or different ideas. They may be reluctant to leave their shells.

4. What may be the cause or basis for these reasons? Identify the things they fear.

5. Coach your people on ways to "stick their necks out" more often so your team will move ahead.

Gem #45

Even if you're on the right track, you'll get run over if you just sit there.

Related Leadership Dimensions:

Focusing on Results

Coaching

Personal Development

Change Management

Innovation

Overview

It takes a lot of work to craft a good strategic direction. This involves extensive industry awareness and competitive analysis, customer research, necessary capital and resources, and an attractive product offering. When all of these factors fall into place, a successful business is born.

However, success can make leaders complacent and arrogant. They may ignore new technology, shifting market forces, or the need to adjust personal leadership styles and views. The same can be said about individual careers. Anyone can become complacent and overlook the need for personal growth and improvement. Without the continual focus to renew and improve one's business and leadership ability, success can easily transition to poor performance and ultimately failure.

Businesses that sustain strong performance are the ones who are constantly moving forward, shunning complacency, and carefully tracking the competition. Even when facing setbacks they never falter. They recognize that they need to sustain their momentum, so they strategically move ahead.

Application

Ask yourself how your organization or team reacts to new or differing ideas. Look at your firm's attitude toward new concepts or modified directions.

One technique is to establish monthly or quarterly improvement meetings when you review the status of the business, competition, and customers. Many successful organizations do this regularly to assess exactly where they stand. Employing brutal honesty is essential as they analyze all relevant data and welcome all inputs. Approach these sessions with a desire to progress and learn, not to maintain the status quo. Avoid the natural tendency of being defensive. Build variety of thought into your leadership team and allow them to question past assumptions.

An open and adaptable approach can help prevent you and your team from getting run over. Complacency is deadly. Together, look for ways to better adapt and quickly respond to shifting needs and circumstances. Success will come to those who never stop improving and looking forward.

Reflection

1. As you take an honest look into your personal development mirror, what do you see? How are you progressing? What concerns you?

2. Do the same to your organization or business. What do you see? How is it progressing?

3. Consider asking a trusted outsider (who brings objectivity) to analyze your career and/or your organization. Can you anticipate what they would tell you? What "complacency" warning signs would they bring to your attention?

4. What type of internal reviews do you regularly hold in your organization to determine your *current* competitiveness AND your readiness for *future* uncertainties?

5. Are you seeking feedback and honest opinions from colleagues and employees about their concerns for the future? As you do so, assure them of no retaliation, and your encouragement for their candor. Are you looking at your organization through the eyes of others?

Gem #46

Remember the
Voice of David:
seek a different
opinion.

Related Leadership Dimensions:

Decision Making

Problem Solving

Ego Management

Listening

Valuing Others

Change Management

Overview

During the middle ages Benedictine monks develped an insightful decision-making approach. When the leader of the monastery was faced with an important decision, he would ask each monk's opinion—starting with the youngest.

The order of questioning was intentional. This tradition was based on a Biblical story involving a young boy named David who volunteered to fight a giant of a man named Goliath. Whoever could beat Goliath would save his nation from being conquered by the enemy. No one was brave enough to fight Goliath, except the small-statured, yet very confident David. The rest cowered at the thought of taking on the feared giant.

David was mocked by the bigger and more seasoned soldiers, yet armed only with a sling, he defeated Goliath and saved his people. Even though all the others knew he would fail, in the end, David was right!

Application

Listening to the Voice of David is a valuable tool in making effective decisions. The next time you need to make an important choice, resist the natural and common tendency of only asking the experts or seasoned leaders for their opinions. While they may provide wise counsel, they may not excel at innovative or non-mainstream opinions.

It often takes a junior or new voice to offer an alternative, contrasting point of view. Poor decisions can come when a leader does not take the time to listen to the "Voice of David". The best answers don't always come from the highest or most senior positions. Seek out different opinions and pay attention to junior, fresher voices.

You might be pleasantly surprised by the alternative points of view that result. And in the process, the new or junior player will appreciate the recognition.

Reflection

1. Think of ways you could improve the overall quality of your work decisions? How often do you seek the opinions of others?

2. To what extent do you solicit the views of newer or younger team members?

3. How often do you follow the natural tendency to only ask for opinions from your trusted colleagues in senior positions with years of experience? You may miss out on new and objective thoughts.

4. Identify the ways in which a fresh perspective can be more objective and beneficial to your team and decision-making processes.

5. To what extent are you willing to intentionally and purposely ask some of your quieter and/or newer employees for their opinions as you consider a critical decision or solve a challenging problem?

Gem #47

Don't sacrifice
the entire war
for the sake
of winning a
single battle.

Related Leadership Dimensions:

Ego Management

Personal Development

Change Management

Overview

Life continuously throws many challenges our way. We try to respond the best we can. When things go our way we feel good. But when they don't, we tend to take emotional action. For example, imagine an executive who feels wronged by a decision or action that affects him adversely. He may perceive it as being unfair.

Overcome with emotion, he marches into his boss's office and lets it fly—telling the boss in no uncertain terms how wrong the boss is, how unfair the decision is, and how angry he feels. He adds a handful of statistics, examples, and figures to prove that the boss is wrong. As he walks away, he smugly congratulates himself on what a brilliant job he just did, how right he was, and that he truly "won that battle!"

Yes, he clearly rubbed his boss's nose in it, and it felt great. And two weeks later, he finds himself reassigned to a remote location where he must oversee an impossible assignment. Pride, emotion, arrogance, and impulsive action cost him dearly and his professional credibility has been tarnished. True, he won the battle, but he lost the war. Impulsive and emotional reactions are usually very costly and damaging in the long-run.

Application

Do you ever face business "battles" that have the potential to destroy you if you insist on "winning"? Be aware of your natural tendencies in moments of conflict or pressure.

Take note of how you manage your emotions or personal ego. Realize that the more emotional a negotiation or discussion becomes, the greater the chance that personal pride can blind you to the larger perspective. Take a break; collect yourself. Sleep on it before you make a decision. Be wary of impulsive choices—those that are made "in the heat of the moment." Seek feedback and don't rely on your perspective alone.

Focusing excessively on specific details to win a single point or battle is a common and normal tendency, but be careful. Develop the attitude that it is better, in the long run, to *lose* some battles. A good leader can make decisions that balance short-term and long-term needs, without sacrificing either. The goal is to win the war, not every battle.

Reflection

1. Critically self-analyze the role that pride, ego, inexperience, and immaturity play in your desire to win every battle you encounter. How can you mitigate these caution flags?

2. Develop a sense of awareness for your level of stress, emotion, or ego—when any of them are high, this is not the time to make a decision. Take a break, slow down. Exhale. Review the situation objectively before you speak or take action.

3. Ask your mentor or coach for guidance based on his or her observations of your tendencies in this area.

4. Place safeguards on your behavior. For instance, establish a rule to never send an emotional or "angry" email/text the same day—write it, leave it, re-read it the next day when you are calm, then determine whether to send it or not.

5. Identify specific situations or people that trigger impulsive or negative feelings and behaviors in you. Train and discipline yourself to avoid "winning" battles that may cost you the war.

Gem #48

Culture is
defined
and
re-defined
every day.

Related Leadership Dimensions:

Personal Integrity
Team Building
Valuing Others
Inspiring Commitment

Overview

Sometimes an organization's culture is described as if it were an object—something you buy or receive. The key to changing a business culture is to recognize that it is what people actually do, not a list of rules on the wall. A healthy culture is not a noun, but a verb.

Far from being an object set in stone, culture is a dynamic, evolving state that begins with the small behaviors that people do every day. Organizational culture is a powerful force that either enables or discourages change. In fact, it is often a company's culture that can be the guilty party when a project stalls or a new idea is attacked. Yet, culture can also provide needed momentum to help achieve desired results.

Culture is defined by the every day behaviors, interactions, attitudes, and values that employees and teams engage in. This includes how they treat each other, deal with their customers, manage change, honor contracts, consider new ideas and approaches, and are true to their word. An organization's culture directly influences its reputation, credibility, and performance.

Application

Recognizing that culture is not a permanent condition presents opportunities to mold it to best support the strategies and attitudes of the business. It needs to be dynamic and evolving rather than static. Culture can be changed. Leaders play a major role in defining <u>and</u> re-defining it every day.

Therefore, cultural change starts with what you, as a leader, do in your daily interactions. Begin paying attention to how you respond to others or describe the business needs to your employees. Each of your behaviors and actions is defining and reinforcing the culture of your organization.

Your culture is the sum total of the way your organization values relationships, treats its customers, carries out negotiations, transacts business, values its people, and all the other daily behaviors, attitudes, and practices that are seen and judged by those inside and outside your business. If you want to improve your organization's culture, change the day-to-day behavior and attitudes of your leaders.

Reflection

1. Ask your people how they define your organization's culture. What would they say? How would they describe what they observe every day?

2. How is your company, team, or group seen by others—both inside and outside the business? How are they regarded in terms of trust, integrity, values, practices, and fairness?

3. If you want to change or alter your current culture, what specific behaviors and attitudes would you work to modify?

4. In shaping your culture, how influential are your most senior positioned leaders? How pervasive are their examples?

5. The actions of an organization's leaders and people are far more influential in defining its culture than words, mottos, lists, posters, ad themes, and pronouncements.

Gem #49

In times of stress, leaders tend to revert to their natural tendencies.

Related Leadership Dimensions:

Focusing on Results

Coaching

Ego Management

Personal Development

Overview

Having taught leadership courses for decades, I have noticed that no matter how intensive the coaching has been to help executives improve their behaviors, in times of stress it seems that leaders often revert back to their original tendencies.

No matter how determined leaders are not to do it, when a crisis hits, too often the training flies out the window and natural inclinations come out loud and clear, and are witnessed by everyone.

This is true about how leaders communicate, build (or hurt) relationships, influence team dynamics, receive criticism, provide corrective feedback, deal with superiors, control their own emotions, and interact with stakeholders. Months can pass with excellent behavior, but once a certain level of stress is reached, individuals are likely to regress and return to what was once instinctively natural and comfortable. And that can be highly destructive to a career and to an organization.

Application

When you see extreme stress coming into your world, be on guard for your natural response patterns to kick into gear.

Plan in advance for how you can prevent these old, counterproductive behaviors from coming into play. Think of how you typically behave in times of conflict and stress. You will likely identify undesirable behaviors that emerge under stress. Consider the feedback you have received in the past from leadership training courses or from your boss and direct reports. What did you learn about your natural tendencies?

Identify behaviors you engage in when there is conflict. Remind yourself of alternative, preferred behaviors. Consider a method to check yourself in challenging and emotional times. This may involve a mentor, peer, or coach. Perhaps you could leave a cryptic note on your screen reminding you how to control your negative behaviors.

Challenging times can sometimes bring out the worst in us, but we can plan ahead and minimize actions that we might later regret.

Reflection

1. Identify any natural, counterproductive behaviors you need to avoid during stressful situations.

2. What experiences have you had that demonstrate that these natural reactions are regrettable?

3. Identify behavior triggers that set off your personal meltdowns so you can sense them coming on and control them—so they don't catch you off-guard.

4. What techniques do you try to employ to react differently, so there are no regrets. Do you use visual reminders, like a sticky note on your screen?

5. Do you have a trusted colleague, mentor, or coach who has helped you with these behaviors before? What was their counsel? You may want to review it again.

Gem #50

Tell them *why*.

Related Leadership Dimensions:

Effective Communication
Delegating
Focusing on Results
Personal Development
Team Building
Inspiring Commitment

Overview

A s a leader, your job is to leverage your capabilities through others because you are limited in time and capacity. A primary piece of this equation is effective delegation. Much has been written and taught on this subject because it is absolutely essential in high quality execution.

An essential phase of delegation is too often either omitted or minimized, with the final result being far from the desired outcome. This key element is making sure leaders tell their people *the why* when giving them a task to perform.

Learning *why* something is to be done gives people essential information about the nature and importance of the task. The "why" provides understanding of the related expectations and the big picture surrounding the request, which directly influences the amount of support and buy-in that your people will commit toward the task's successful achievement.

Application

Your organization or department is likely overloaded with assignments, projects, and targets. Improving your delegation skills is an important method of managing activities, budgets, and schedules.

For example, the next time you have a critical task to be performed, and you obviously have no time to do it yourself, carefully determine who you believe is best suited to complete it. Then, as you explain what needs to be done, share *why* the task is important. Express what is at stake and who will be affected. Avoid the mind trap that suggests that withholding knowledge of the "why" increases your own power and control. In truth, it is the opposite.

Your sharing of information will help them feel that you trust them. Consequently, they will put more meaning and emphasis into completing the delegated task because they know why it is important. They need to know what is behind the assignment. If they know they will perform at a much higher level. Sharing the *why* will create a win-win for you and your people.

Overview

Employees need feedback on performance to grow and improve, and to know how their performance is viewed by their boss. Positive feedback is usually easy to give. However, one of the most difficult things for a leader to do *well*, is give appropriate corrective feedback to an employee or team member.

A frequent mistake made by leaders is correcting the employee in front of others. Few things will demean one's dignity so quickly as being criticized openly, especially in front of one's peers. This may cause deep emotional wounds because their pride and dignity have been attacked—even though they may not outwardly show it.

When criticizing someone publicly, it may not be obvious that the person is wounded, but it is felt on the inside, even by the most jaded of individuals. The likely result is decreased commitment by the employee to both the task and the leader.

Application

Sharing appropriate corrective feedback must not be ignored. It is essential for the growth and progress of both the person and the organization. But, the place and timing of giving such feedback is important to avoid embarrassment by the receiver.

Waiting a few minutes for a time when you can talk calmly and privately to the employee will allow you to rationally and effectively teach the appropriate behavior while allowing them to maintain their dignity. When you give the feedback, remember to be specific, focus on the behavior, and don't belittle or attack the person. Refrain from producing a laundry list of past mistakes. Instead, focus on the current situation. Turn it into a learning session.

As a result, your people will be more receptive to your instruction and more inclined to modify their behavior because they will feel valued as a person. *How* and *when* you handle corrective feedback has a huge impact on your people's response to it, and their future behavior and attitude.

Reflection

1. Even though it is difficult, and easily procrastinated, do you give appropriate corrective feedback when it is needed?

2. How have *you* felt when a supervisor corrected you in front of your peers? You likely felt embarrassed or put on the spot. Your people are no different. They have similar feelings.

3. How well do you reject the myth that some people don't mind being corrected in front of their peers? Some of them may wear a stoic poker face, but their pride, ego, and reputation are just as vulnerable as anyone else's.

4. How much attention do you pay to the timing of corrective feedback? Do you wait until you can be alone with the person, without waiting too long? Feedback should be done within a day or two or the impact and coaching opportunity is significantly diminished.

5. To what extent do you grasp the importance of helping each of your team members maintain their dignity and self-worth? There are many ways that an individual's level of dignity is correlated to their level of performance.

Gem #52

A coil pulled
too tight loses
its spring.

Related Leadership Dimensions:

Focusing on Results

Personal Development

Time Management

Overview

B usy professionals have a high potential of experiencing burnout as they manage their daily demands. This constant flood of challenging and unanticipated issues influence their behavior and can contribute to unhealthy amounts of stress.

With a desire to achieve success, especially when under heavy pressure, a leader may mistakenly conclude that the best response is to increase intensity—both with time and output. However, this unbalanced approach, maintained over time, will likely produce detrimental effects for the leader and the team—resulting in negative impacts on the quality of their decisions and performance.

For example, busy professionals who keep delaying long overdue vacations will likely see their effectiveness suffer. This is primarily due to their excessive stress and tension that also has a debilitating effect on their relationships and quality of work. Much like a coil that is pulled too tightly, leaders who maintain continuous stress and strain will risk losing their ability to achieve stellar results.

Application

Reflect on your daily and weekly schedule. In spite of all your pressures, activities, and commitments, you need some personal downtime.

Finding ways to cope with stress and the constant rhythm of business is essential to staying effective. Identify activities that are rejuvenating to you. Seek out people who bring a relaxing smile to your face. Note how often you laugh during the day. Vacations are a vital means of relaxing and releasing pressure. Weekends away from work can improve perspectives and bring freshness. You need mental and emotional breaks. Alternate your focus. Consider these needed breaks as a vital tune-up to ensure strong future performance.

These informal actions are not a waste of time, but a valuable technique to increase your energy, stamina, and focus during the times that are the most critical. It will also have a positive influence on your team by reducing their stress.

Vary your intensity to sustain your effectiveness as a leader. Loosen your coil a notch or two and you will be more flexible, effective, *and* healthy.

Reflection

1. Ask a trusted colleague for their observations of your typical stress level.

2. Are you capable of making your best decisions when you are working under extreme or prolonged stress?

3. What types of physical activities do you engage in to help manage your stress more effectively? What additional methods could you use? How can you let go of work pressures?

4. What signals (from your body, mind, or environment) alert you that you are under excessive stress? Do you believe stress can be detrimental to your effectiveness and happiness?

5. Did you know that regular exercise has a positive correlation to the quality of your sleep, which directly affects your mental alertness, decision-making, interpersonal relations, and the nonverbal signals you emit to your associates and customers?

Index

Introduction to Index

The following index is organized by the four quadrants of the LEAD NOW! model and the 21 Leadership Dimensions. The *Leadership Gems* are listed under the Dimensions to which the Gem relates. Connecting the Leadership Gems to the LEAD NOW! model will help you develop a personal comprehensive leadership development strategy.

LEAD NOW! MODEL
21 Leadership Dimensions

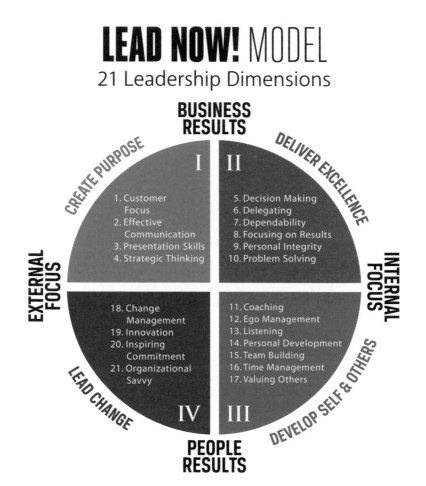

BUSINESS RESULTS

CREATE PURPOSE

DELIVER EXCELLENCE

EXTERNAL FOCUS

INTERNAL FOCUS

I

1. Customer Focus
2. Effective Communication
3. Presentation Skills
4. Strategic Thinking

II

5. Decision Making
6. Delegating
7. Dependability
8. Focusing on Results
9. Personal Integrity
10. Problem Solving

IV

18. Change Management
19. Innovation
20. Inspiring Commitment
21. Organizational Savvy

III

11. Coaching
12. Ego Management
13. Listening
14. Personal Development
15. Team Building
16. Time Management
17. Valuing Others

LEAD CHANGE

DEVELOP SELF & OTHERS

PEOPLE RESULTS

Quadrant I: Create Purpose

(Externally Focused Business Results)

A leader is responsible for defining the group's vision and strategy. Creating Purpose identifies what the organization stands for, what it is going to do, and how it is positioned in the marketplace. This involves studying the competition, knowing the customer, analyzing industry trends, setting strategy, and communicating effectively to others.

Quadrant II: Deliver Excellence

(Internally Focused Business Results)

A leader is responsible for delivering operational excellence—translating the strategy into day-to-day execution for the organization. This involves clear decision-making, the ability to build consistent and measurable processes, continuous improvement, and behaving with integrity.

Quadrant III: Develop Self & Others

(Internally Focused People Results)

A leader must value learning for him/herself and for others. This involves seeking personal improvement opportunities, building and managing team dynamics, honing technical expertise, managing one's time, coaching and developing others, and managing one's ego.

Quadrant IV: Lead Change

(Externally Focused People Results)

A leader is responsible for creating and championing change efforts that will benefit the organization. This involves influencing key decision makers, sponsoring change projects, empowering stakeholders, encouraging innovation, managing resistance, and making change stick.

Quadrant I: Create Purpose

1. Customer Focus
2. Effective Communication
3. Presentation Skills
4. Strategic Thinking

Quadrant II: Deliver Excellence

5. Decision Making
6. Delegating
7. Dependability
8. Focusing on Results
9. Personal Integrity
10. Problem Solving

Quadrant III: Develop Self & Others

11. Coaching
12. Ego Management
13. Listening
14. Personal Development
15. Team Building
16. Time Management
17. Valuing Others

Quadrant IV: Lead Change

18. Change Management
19. Innovation
20. Inspiring Commitment
21. Organizational Savvy

Index by Leadership Dimension

Ego Management (Develop Self & Others)

Focusing on Results (Deliver Excellence)

Listening (Develop Self & Others)

Organizational Savvy (Lead Change)

Personal Development (Develop Self & Others)

Personal Integrity (Deliver Excellence)

——•——

Team Building (Develop Self & Others)

Author

John Parker Stewart

John is an internationally recognized executive coach, leadership and organization consultant, sought-after speaker, national award winning trainer, orals coach for government contractors, and author. Over the past 35 years, he has coached and trained tens of thousands of leaders worldwide. He specializes in team performance, executive development, change management, and leadership training. He managed executive and leadership development for 86,000 employees at Lockheed Corp where he designed and taught the Lockheed Executive Institutes for

13 years. He started Stewart Systems, Inc. in 1980, where he has researched, consulted, taught, and coached thousands of leaders—CEOs, presidents, executives, and managers—including all levels of management at Kennedy Space Center over an eight year period.

After attending the University of Colorado, John received his bachelor's degree from Brigham Young University. He completed his master's degree in Organizational Communication and wrote his thesis in London, with additional graduate work and teaching at Michigan State University. He performed more graduate studies under management guru Peter Drucker at Claremont Graduate School. John was selected "National Trainer of the Year" by the American Society for Training and Development for two consecutive years.

He has researched organizations and worked with corporations worldwide. His client list includes NASA, Lockheed Martin, Citibank, Toshiba, Xerox, Chevron, Raytheon, CSL-Hong Kong, GM, Shell Oil-Malaysia, Kaiser Permanente, Telstra-Australia, US Air Force, US Dept of Energy, Kennedy Space Center, Boeing, IBM, Rockwell, BAE Systems, TVA, Duke Energy, Northrop Grumman, and many other government agencies and commercial firms.

John resides in Lake Oswego, Oregon.

Visit his website: www.johnparkerstewart.com